THE PELICAN LATIN AMERICAN LIBRARY
Editor: Richard Gott

Cambão – The Yoke

Francisco Julião was born in Pernambuco State in
North-East Brazil. He spent his childhood amongst some
of the most wretched peasantry of Latin America, and his
experiences inspired him with radical ideas which he
attempted to put into practice after he left the Recife law
school in 1939. For fifteen years he laboured as a peasants'
lawyer to defend tenants and labourers against the region's
latifundios and sugar refineries. Then, in 1955, he
organized the first Peasant League on a former cane
plantation near Recife. Thanks to his long familiarity with
the peasantry he managed to create a vast movement
which united hundreds of thousands of peasants
throughout the region. Soon the league was campaigning
for radical agrarian reform and was in conflict with the
army and state police forces. With the military coup of
April 1964 it was suppressed.

In 1964 Francisco Julião was exiled and now lives in Mexico
in close contact with the illegal Peasant Leagues in Brazil.

Cambão-The Yoke

The Hidden Face
of Brazil

Francisco Julião
Translated by John Butt

Penguin Books

Penguin Books Ltd, Harmondsworth,
Middlesex, England
Penguin Books Inc., 7110 Ambassador Road,
Baltimore, Maryland 21207, U.S.A.
Penguin Books Australia Ltd, Ringwood,
Victoria, Australia

Published in Pelican Books 1972
Translation copyright © John Butt, 1972

Made and printed in Great Britain by
Hazell Watson & Viney Ltd
Aylesbury, Bucks
Set in Linotype Juliana

This book is sold subject to the condition that
it shall not, by way of trade or otherwise, be lent,
re-sold, hired out, or otherwise circulated without
the publisher's prior consent in any form of
binding or cover other than that in which it is
published and without a similar condition
including this condition being imposed on the
subsequent purchaser

Contents

Editorial Preface – John Butt	7
Introduction – A word	11

Part 1 – Beginning Life

Roots	17
Childhood and the Countryside	27
Passion and the North-East	33

Part 2 – Encounter With the Peasant

The Peasant and Humanity	49
Religion, *Cachaça, Capanga*	58
The Peasant of the North-East	64
An Ideological Word	69

Part 3 – The Peasant League

The North-East and the League	87
The League and the Law	104
The Beginnings of Resistance	113
Collective Resistance	124
The League and the Army	136
The League and the Church	148
The League and the Unions	156

Part 4 – Encounter With America

A Wider Vision	173
Index	182

Editorial Preface

This book was written for Brazilians, and the following historical note may help orientate English-speaking readers.

Brazil was an independent empire based on black slavery until 1889 – slavery was abolished in 1888. The Republic was inaugurated in 1889 by a military coup led by Floriano Peixoto and Deodoro, and democracy of a sort was maintained until a right-wing take-over in 1930 installed Getulio Vargas as dictator on an anti-communist platform. Vargas was toppled in 1945 by a liberal-oriented military coup – to return as president ('Brazil's Perón') until his suicide in 1955. Kubitschek, with the left-wing Goulart as vice-president, then began a period of reform which disturbed Washington and was accompanied by galloping inflation of the *cruzeiro*. The Peasant League and other popular movements were founded this year in the new, progressive atmosphere. In 1960 Quadros defeated the progressive nationalist Teixeira Lott, and a conservative reaction began; though Quadros resigned in 1961 in favour of Goulart who had support among socialists and communists. A plan of agrarian reform was initiated and other reformist policies attempted. In 1963 Marshal Tito visited Brazil and this worsened relations with Washington and the military in Brazil.

In April 1964, in defence of 'Christian values and order', a C.I.A.-inspired military coup ousted Goulart and opened a period of rule by decree. Popular movements were suppressed (including Julião's Peasant League), and left-wingers were exiled or jailed. Free political parties and legal opposition have never since returned to Brazil.

*

Portuguese consonants are pronounced as in French; the vowels as in Spanish or Italian. Final 'e' is almost mute, *ão* is like the English ow and *ãe* like eye.

J.B.

'A militant's weapon is his humanity'
– Jean Paul Sartre

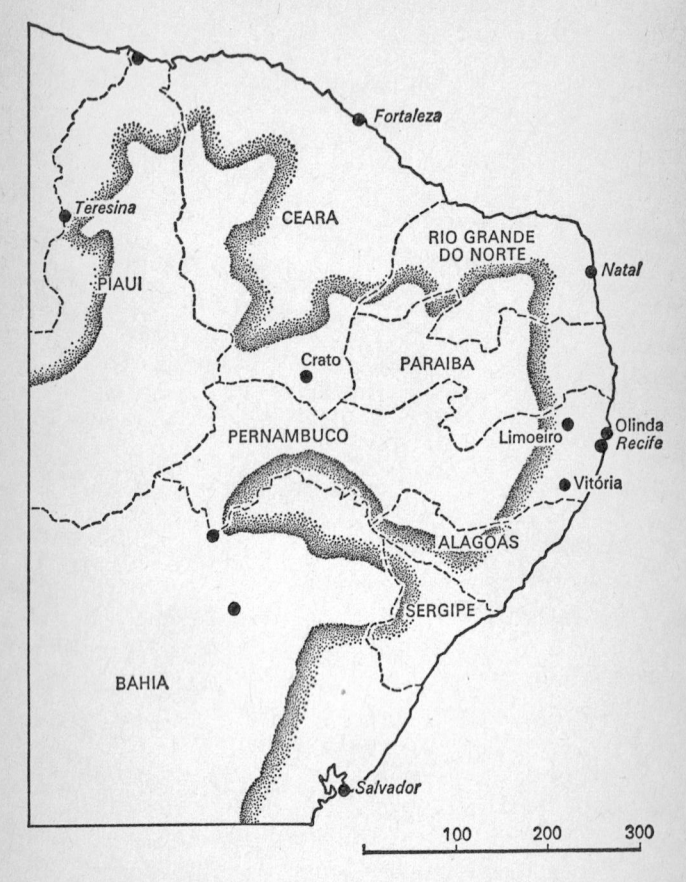

The Brazilian North-East. The shaded line indicates the limit of the *sertão* or highlands. The coastal strip is called the *mata*, and the intermediate zone the *agreste*.

Introduction
A Word

Cambão. A spark setting the countryside ablaze; a match under a charge as old as the peasant or slave himself; and a word signalling the start of a long and arduous journey. In every language in the world it has many names, and each means slavery. I don't intend to investigate the precise origins of the institution of slavery or to trace its development in time and space. That alone would need a volume. Nor am I even interested in tracing its course in the Brazilian North-East where it is called *cambão*; let alone in this endless vastness of the land of Brazil where it changes name from place to place, and even from *latifundio** to *latifundio*, like the criminal and outlaw it always was and will be.

In the North-East, in the cassava and sugar-cane zone, *cambão* is the name given to the dry, leafless and earless maize stalk. It also refers to the piece of wood hung round an ox's neck and trailing between his legs to slow his pace. It means the yoke fixed to the shaft with raw leather thongs; the *boi-de-cambão* or yoke-ox is the one who walks in front pushing the yoke; the *boi-de-coice* follows behind holding up the shaft. Finally, *cambão* is the day's unpaid labour demanded by landowners once a week from their peasants as rent for their land – normally a miserable patch of one or two hectares if the tenant is a day labourer or hired hand. In the

* A *Latifundio* is a large estate in which considerable tracts of land are held in reserve, almost as if it were capital.

case of a tenant farmer, *cambão* is labour given free to the owners at certain times of the year in addition to the usual rent in money or kind.

It's no surprise that *cambão*, the dry, leafless maize stalk good only for burning, should give its name to the useless labour offered up by the peasants to placate the gods of this world. Nor is it unfitting that the name should also derive from the yoke which ties the ox to the shaft, just as the hoe ties the peasant for life to land which he does not even own, in contradiction of all the laws of nature. But to speak only of animals: yoke-ox and landless peasant lead the same lives, bound, staggering, worn down by a task which only finishes for one in the slaughter-house and for the other in the grave.

Cambão, cambaio, cambeta, cambado, cambo, cambembe, cambito, cambada: look in the dictionary and you find that every variant signifies some misfortune – 'gang', 'crippled', 'bandy-legged', 'limbless' – except the fundamental one: labour not even rewarded with bread and water. And this points sadly to the fact that even dictionaries omit things out of fear of or in league with the *latifundio*.

The *cambão* is where it all begins. The end will be the final and absolute destruction of the *latifundio* so that not a root or a seed or a germ is left whence it might sprout again and regain its power. For this is how it has always been.

Cambão was the spark which fired the Peasant League in the North-East. Hence the title of this book, which offers no general theories about man or the land, but hopes to expose the hidden face of a decadent society choking under the weight of a system based on the *latifundio* and supported by capitalism with foreign aid: a system which history has left behind; a system like an enormous, vile tumour repugnant to any conscience open to the world and the light.

For where *cambão* flourishes men decay. Between the sea-coast where they are more dead than alive, and the *sertão* with its drought-stunted forests and arid plains, men struggle obstinately and hopelessly not so much with the land as with its owners. And now these owners are growing daily more intangible and indefinable as they merge into the anonymous persons of the State and the Law, those diabolical inventions of capitalism.

Not that such a state of affairs is peculiar to the Brazilian North-East. The North-East is rather a microcosm of Latin America with its violent contrasts and single underlying problem: the rigidly-defended monopoly of the sources of natural wealth and the means of working them held by a minority. Latin America is the Brazilian North-East on a continental scale; and like the yoke-ox or the enslaved peasant it continues to suffer from age-old wrongs. The boss may change his name but the cause remains: the *latifundio*. And life where it rules is always the same: slavery, pillage, theft – in a word CAMBÃO!

PART ONE

Beginning Life

CHAPTER 1

Roots

I was born and bred in the traditions of Catholicism, and Christianity gave my life its bearings; but in my home region the landowners look on me as the anti-christ or the apocalyptic beast. My mother, a fervent Catholic who worshipped all the mystics canonized by the church, called her eight children after saints and christened her three daughters Mary. Not content with this she gave all her sons a second name after the saint of their day of birth. My saint was Juliano, but though I was registered under that name I always called myself Julião after I started first school – at which time I knew nothing of the more famous Juliano, the apostate Roman Emperor.

What remains in the long run is the memory of my mother and the gentle mysticism which made her choose holy names for her children in the hope that Christian vigilance and motherly care would make their lives a bed of flowers. I know her stoical tears would have been amply recompensed if at her deathbed her eyes had been closed by a nun-daughter or a son in priest's robes. But she was never to have that consolation: the only Mary who might have given it to her was carried off years before with her virgin's crown and mystical dreams. And those sons who never rebelled against the social order never came to accept it either.

My father died from the press reports of my 'assassination'. I shall always remember him for his straightness and firm principles. I recall one of the lessons he taught us when he could still gather us together round the long table at home. 'If one of you finds a wallet full of money by the roadside, don't pick it up because that might make you want to keep it. Leave it there.' When you're eight years old and soft as clay, a good modeller can fashion you into all sorts of fine and permanent shapes. Now when I recall his advice about the wallet I wonder whether it may have been a decisive source of my life-long contempt for money. As a lawyer I defended nearly every one of my cases free of charge; and the only time I ever signed a contract I tore it up in front of my client because he mentioned it inopportunely. On another occasion a lady whom I had successfully defended forgot to bring me the fees she had herself spontaneously offered to pay me. She started avoiding me in the street, turning corners and slipping into doorways; and one day, when I had had enough, I hurried over to her and said 'Madam, don't bother about the fees. Money's the only thing that'll never make me an enemy. Only injustice will do that.'

This and other radical lessons of my father's against half-truth, ambiguity and compromise must have influenced my own development as a radical. I stress radical and not sectarian. The difference is clear enough but some people confuse the two out of ignorance or malice. Radicalism has a single dimension: man. Its scope is the whole of history and its objective is freedom. But sectarianism is hedgehog-like, self-enclosed and defensive. Radicalism seeks out truth and the centre of things, has a philosophy and dialectic. It seeks confrontation, accepts dialogue and participation. But sectarianism is monologue, isolation, exclusion, intolerance and extremism. Radicalism is love and opens men's eyes; sectarianism inflames passions and blinds. Radicalism discovers man, seeks to identify itself with him, and is intransigent in its attempt to save him. But sectarianism is self-obsessed, impatient and impulsive. Proletarian ideology is radical, but the petty-bourgeois is sectarian. Christianity is basically radical, but the Inquisition is sectarian. The French Revolution is radical, but the Terror was sectarian; and Marxism is radical while the left-wing extremism diagnosed by Lenin as an infantile disorder of communism is a sectarian thing.

Socrates was a radical because he did not yield before the threat of hemlock; neither did Christ before the cross. Saint Paul was a radical when faced with the might of Caesar, and so was Joan of Arc on her pyre. Radicalism made Saint Francis of Assisi despise wealth and made Anthony of Egypt give his belongings to the poor. Brother Caneca* before the firing squad, Tiradentes† on the gallows and Cuauhtemoc on his 'bed of roses' – all these were radicals. When the Americans fought for their independence they took a radical decision, and George Washington emerged then as a symbol of radicalism because he would not yield to England. Bolívar, San Martín, Sucre, Morelos, Bonifácio, Artigas, O'Higgins, all were radicals in their struggle for South America against the Peninsula, because they stood by their faith.

As soon as some seed takes root in consciousness life struggles to thrust it deep in search of life-giving moisture. Other factors combined with my father's teachings to strengthen my growing radicalism, and I shall mention them later; but first I must speak of my grandparents to complete the picture I hope to draw in this chapter of the experiences which entitle me to speak on the subject of this book.

My paternal grandfather died in the year that I was born, but left me his name and his dreams. This obscure captain, who owned much land and over a hundred slaves, comes high on the list of men who influenced me, and I heard stories

*Caneca was shot as a result of a revolutionary attempt in March 1817.

†'Toothpuller', J. José da Silva, popular revolutionary from Minas Gerais who took part in an abortive uprising in 1789.

about him which – added to my father's teachings – played their part in forming my character and putting my feet on a road which led inevitably to socialism.

He owned one of the region's biggest sugar plantations, called Boa Esperança or Good Hope, with a sixty-tube boiler of English make and a chimney eighty palms high, as well as rich land full of forests and springs which he toured from time to time on a fine horse. During such tours he would frequently come across a clearing with a mud hut, fruit-patch and a plot of cassava and maize where an unfamiliar negro or half-caste would be quietly bent over his hoe with his wife and children beside him. The dialogue between master and tenant was always the same.

'What are these lands called, friend?'

'They belong to "Espera".'

(The people never called the place Boa Esperança but 'Espera', after a pool shaded with andira trees, one of the best hunting places in the region.)

'And who's the owner?'

'Captain Francisco de Paula.'

'By the look of your house and fruit-patch you've been here some time ...'

'Five years.'

'D'you pay rent?'

'Not yet.'

'Are you attached to the estate then?'

'No.'

'Then you live here free ...?'

'I do and I don't. I haven't been to see the Captain about the rent, that's all.'

'So you haven't paid rent for five years?'

'That's right. Every year I say to myself, I'll go and see him, and then I leave it ...'

'What about the Captain ...?'

'I don't know him myself, but they all tell me he's as good as gold and won't hurt poor people.'

'And how did you come here then?'

'I was running away from the plantation. It was slavery there.'

'Well don't spend another five years waiting to talk to the Captain.'

'Are you the Captain then...?'

'Who knows, you might be talking to him...'

And then he would spur his horse and ride off. Like all big landowners he used to ride with a servant who fixed his stirrups and did all the other chores forbidden my grandfather by age and social position, and I met one of them who was with him to the last, an eighty-year-old of remarkable memory who told me the following story. One evening as he was riding back to the house after a trip to his estate the servant saw a man cutting cane. As it was outside harvesttime and the man had no time to hide, he called to his master who was riding in front: 'Captain, So-and-So's stealing cane.' The Captain didn't even slow his horse or turn round, but simply murmured: 'Pretend you didn't see him. He planted that cane himself.'

Grandfather was a fervent supporter of Joaquim Nabuco the abolitionist; and he once made him welcome in his home at a time when other landowners were calling him a lunatic communist unfit to set foot in a decent household. He was also unique in a region entirely given to sugar-cane farming. When after more than a century's campaigning the *Lei Aurea* or Golden Law was finally passed on 13 May 1888 with its two articles abolishing black slavery in Brazil, my grandfather assembled the slaves in the yard and showed them the telegram with the news.

'You're free now. You can go where you like and take your wives and children too.'

One of the oldest slaves stepped forward.

'What if folks want to stay on? Is it all right?'

'Yes, but not as slaves.'

'Let's go on how we were, Captain. There's no whipping or stocks here, and blacks can't get rich anyway ...'

'But it's different now. Everybody can work for whom he likes, and you can go round the country wherever you want.'

Next day the same negro came and asked for my grandfather.

'Captain, everyone wants to stay.'

'Then all you have to do is find a place and put up your hut. There's no shortage of land.'

And so they did.

Meanwhile most of the other big plantation-owners in the area lost all their black slaves overnight; many were ruined and some committed suicide as a result of their loss. I met some of these slaves, by then white-haired – 'a negro with white hair must be more than ninety' the saying goes – who talked of grandfather with tears in their eyes. The granddaughter of one of these slaves, Bernardina, was my wet-nurse and I shall never forget her. She was tall, slim, calm, with the soft eyes and voice, slow movements, and straight upright walk I saw years later in Senegal when I first trod the soil of Africa and felt the heat of the Sahara on my face.

It was this Senegalese who told me of my grandfather's death. Just before he died he asked them to carry him to the plantation fields where he lay thin and silent, watching the cane being milled. The news that the Captain had come to say good-bye fell across the fields like a dark shadow. They all stopped work and stood before him; the boilerman shut off the steam and the crushers fell silent; and then my grandfather began to weep, and so did the sons and grandsons of the old slaves. They took him back to the house where he died peacefully, 'like a bird died of sadness in his cage', my nurse used to say. Three days later they saw a line of ants marching into his bedroom, drawn by his old cap which was sweet with the old man's sweat (he was a diabetic). The people there used to say the Captain was 'sweet as sugar. Even the ants loved him'.

My mother's father was called Manoel Tertuliano Travassos de Arruda, and was a short, red-faced man with a shining bald pate and white, pointed goatee. He had been a magistrate and was famous as a lawyer as well as devoted to politics. He always talked in a shout, and was a rich landowner – he had even more land than my other grandfather. He lived with his twenty-six children from two marriages in an ancient *casa grande* with a veranda and wooden steps in front. Opposite the house, which is still called Pasassunga, was the sugar mill driven by a horse tied to a long pole, and on the left was the church where the family attended mass. Behind was the graveyard where master and slave met their similar fates. Every January the festival of Saint Sebastian was held in the courtyard in front of the church, and this lasted ten days and drew thousands of spectators.

My mother used to call the children together and order the best ox-cart with wooden seats padded with cushions stuffed with cane leaves, and a cover on top made of rush mats lined with best cloth in gay colours. Then we would ride squeakily along the two-league road to Pasassunga, driven by a carter with a shining whip which never touched the animals' flanks, while father rode beside on a sorrel. The journey took ages.

My grandfather was an archetypal feudal lord, and liked to stand on the top balcony of his house shouting down at his servants who would gather, hat in hand, with their faces turned respectfully upwards. His great luxury was a twenty-four piece orchestra made up of his own children and some of the closest servants in the *casa grande*. Despite all this worldly success and his being a magistrate, only the oldest son took up law, and he went to live in the state of Pará in north Brazil where he married and made a career as an appeal judge. I can remember Uncle Abdias clearly – short, red-faced and frail – the day he came back to Pernambuco at the age of eighty and knelt sobbing to kiss the land where he had been born, quoting the famous lines 'As the bird returns to his former nest' in self-justification.

The other children lived on with their father, marrying and setting up on his land until the old man died and the family dispersed. Many wasted their share of the legacy and were ruined; most made for the cities and took jobs as drivers, bakers or insurance agents, or joined the army or navy. Nearly all the daughters were married off, although they could barely write their own names – as was usual even in the early years of this century. They were sought after because they knew how to run a household and cook, and could saddle a horse as well as they played the violin or danced the waltz.

When Floriano Peixoto, justly named the 'Iron Marshal' and 'Defender of the State', took power from the ineffectual hands of Marshal Deodoro de Fonsêca,* he nominated the heroic Captain Barbosa Lima as Governor of Pernambuco.

During Barbosa Lima's period of government an incident occurred which nearly landed my grandfather in jail. A band of thieves stole twelve of his best riding horses, but was captured, brought to the house and locked in the old slave yard or *senzala*. While grandfather was preparing a case against them before handing them over to the authorities, his young sons conspired with the watchmen guarding the prisoners to brand a letter L for *ladrão* or thief on the suspects' faces. The last of the poor wretches let out such a scream of agony that he alerted the household and grandfather discovered this new

---

*Peixoto and Deodoro led the republican coup against Pedro II in 1889. Deodoro was incompetent and Peixoto overthrew him in 1892 – to be overthrown himself in 1894.

crime committed by his own sons. He decided however to accept responsibility and to hand the thieves over to the authorities; but the news spread and his political enemies started a press campaign against him.

Even though grandfather was on Barbosa Lima's side in politics, the latter was compelled to send an officer and fifty men to arrest him on his own estate – although he made sure the move was so well publicized that grandfather had plenty of time to make a getaway. But even his prestige as a magistrate and politician didn't spare him a costly law case, and he had to spend fifty thousand *mil-reis* in his own defence at a time when a thousand *mil-reis* would buy a herd of cattle and a good stretch of land. He avoided a jail sentence but remained unjustly notorious as a brander of thieves – a notoriety he could have escaped had he followed the advice of the Governor himself: 'Dr Arruda's mistake was that he failed to do what every herdsman does when branding: let the animals go afterwards.'

I tell this story to show how things were beginning to change for the big landowners like my grandfather after Abolition and the advent of the republic. Before those things none of this could have happened, even if the crime had been a deliberate atrocity by the bailiffs or foremen or even the owner himself, and not the action of a gang of irresponsible youths.

In those days before Abolition a horse was worth as much as a slave, and even rose in value afterwards – at least until the roads were good enough for the first cars. Life was impossible without a horse or mule to bring the cotton, castor beans and leather down from the *sertão* to be changed for cloth, sugar or other lowland articles. Ranch- and plantation-owners alike rode on horseback, as did their wives; and horses turned the cane crushers, pulled the carriages, and on festival days went to rodeos and races. They were more important than cannons in wartime, and are still used to patrol the cities. No one – except slaves or serfs who had nothing save their hide aprons – would move an inch except on horseback or in a carriage trotting or galloping along as they pleased. One dismounted only to eat, rest or make love. The rest – work, travel, courting, marriage, business, herding, celebrating, hunting, funerals and war – all was done on horseback.

Nevertheless horse thieves could still find a protector or 'fence' who might easily be a respectable citizen or powerful landowner. In our area the most notorious of these 'fences' was for many years a local political boss, a cunning Portuguese who laid down the law with a hangman's noose and machete. All the same if a horse thief was caught he suffered death and was executed by the bailiffs or stewards with a dagger or shotgun. One landowner, who was later killed by his own son in a dispute over the inheritance, was particularly renowned for his savagery with such criminals. In days when big landowners had absolute power and an obstinate gatekeeper held more sway over the local police than a habeas corpus from some easily-removed magistrate, this particular owner would punish his thieves by himself taking a red-hot iron and thrusting it into the prisoner's anus to burn out his guts. None of his victims escaped this dreadful torture which went unpunished in a society which considered theft more serious than homicide. The fact is that since man has become a wolf to his fellows on account of the institution of property, the latter has been more valuable than life, family and country put together.

CHAPTER 2

Childhood and the Countryside

Tales about their ancestors make an indelible impression on the minds of young children, and there are few who don't yearn to follow in the footsteps of a grandfather whom they have turned into a romantic legend. This romantic figure grows with time till the child begins to confuse him with story-book heroes. But nearer relatives like a father or living grandfather shrink in stature because their reality is known: a child magnifies their faults just as he magnifies the virtues of someone known only through pictures or anecdotes. We all have a special place in our hearts for a father or grandfather endowed with some special quality which imagination can exaggerate and idolize; and there is a plantation-owner lurking in the heart of any of his grandsons. I was no exception to this rule which I suppose I have confirmed by choosing my father's father as a model.

Life often works against such influences and guides us along paths away from or even against the figures we admire. But if I'm candid with myself I have to admit I would have been very much like that grandfather had I lived in his times and been bound by the same social status, wealth and customs.

My childhood was spent in the shadow of the enormous chimney he built. Of his immense estates half remained at his death, and this half was divided into nine equal portions one of which went to my father. By adding his own savings to mother's legacy he bought one of his sisters' portions, and later on he rented land from the youngest son and farmed these lands for the next twenty years. It was good land which would take any crop, but father was still obliged to raise money by other means to keep up his income. Sugar prices were dropping yearly, and I remember him sending off one load and the carters returning empty-handed because the price didn't even cover the transportation costs.

I was born on a plantation in Pernambuco just when the rise of the big sugar refineries was pushing my father into decline. It would take a whole book to tell of my first thirteen years on the plantation, and of the chores of sugar farming, the cutting and planting of demerara, *cristalina*, *flor de Cuba* and other special high-juice varieties; and of the harvesting and crushing, sugar-boiling and rum-distilling which make up life in such places. But this isn't my intention. However I must mention the distance that separated tenants and hands from their masters on those plantations; a distance which grew as the owners' financial situation worsened, and which was inherited by the sons who tried to increase it as though it were a birthright or an investment for the future.

As long as the sugar plantations were economically strong, the owners had political power and the sugar region was decisive in the country's politics. Bad roads and slow communications on foot or horseback obliged planters to live on their land with their families and to build a church or chapel near by as well as a cemetery and to mix with their own tenants. Tenants were divided into three categories: *eiteiros* or labourers, cane-growers and tenant farmers. As the daily business of sugar farming needs a certain amount of specialized knowledge, there was always a bare half dozen skilled men such as carpenters, boilermen, blacksmiths, sugarmen, masons and stillmen. Some planters took tutors or governesses for their children, and some even hired a chaplain to say mass and teach Latin. I've already mentioned my grandfather who kept a whole orchestra to play him marches and waltzes.

The plantation was thus an enclosed, semi-feudal society where the *casa grande* became the castle and the tenants were more or less serfs who did nothing without their lord's consent; and life passed monotonously and, at least on the surface, harmoniously. The peasants (the word took long to establish itself in Brazil, and more of its ideological significance later) looked on the master as a father appointed to punish and protect them. Punishment consisted of obligations like the 'service days' (which might take up a whole week including Sunday) for planting, washing and crushing cane. Hours were measured by the sun: six till six for ordinary labourers. Tenant farmers paid *cambão*, the medieval *corvée* or unpaid labour, on top of the rent or *fôro* which was agreed by verbal contract and – in the North-East – traditionally paid once a year on 8 December, Conception Day.*

The master granted his protection in return for absolute obedience, and this protection consisted of defence from the police or law when the tenant or peasant had committed violence, murder or some other crime not dishonourable to the master's good name. If the master wasn't strong enough to harbour a criminal – as happened when he was in opposition to the ruling political party – there was always some friend or relation who would take in the peasant and thus win the master's political support. There was one permanent rule however: a man who had fulfilled his obligations for many years would still find it hard to get a place on another estate unless he had references from his previous master proving he had paid rent regularly and abandoned his land with the owner's consent. The only exception to this rule was when

*The Catholic feast-day celebrating the immaculate conception of Mary.

the owners involved had fallen out over some dispute over family, land or politics.

Abolition shook this society from top to bottom. The republic was another blow. But what really broke it was the refineries and their modern equipment which could reduce a load of cane to syrup in hours where a plantation would have had to work for months.

Refinery sugar was white, crystalline and pure, and was sold abroad under international agreements and state protection. It was a much-needed source of money to create new wealth and cover the state's growing foreign debt. Plantation sugar was dark and coarse and took days or weeks to harden out in the old zinc or wood moulds before it was sold to packers and refiners. It never got further than the local markets where it was eaten by poor peasants in coconut and rice candies on fiesta days.

The new sugar refineries reduced the plantations to obsolescence, and one by one the old boilers were left unlit and days dawned undisturbed by the shriek of their whistles.

The story of the decline and fall of the sugar aristocracy has been told by the novelist José Lins do Rêgo who, like me and all the children of that and the following generation, witnessed the twilight of the north-eastern sugar plantations and the rise of the refineries which swallowed up the land and ruined the old patriarchal families. Their descendants now vegetated in the *casas grandes*, where the old men wandered like melancholy ghosts while the children fled to the cities and to new ways of life. The refinery-owners were shrewd and ruthless like all capitalists. With an eye on the still-fertile valleys and hills of the region, they lent money to needy landowners in return for mortgages or sale contracts which were either renewed with added interest or produced in court, which meant the speedy arrival of the bailiff and the definitive loss of the estate for the heirs.

Childhood and the Countryside 31

Differences between heirs were common and the refinery-owners played on them cleverly, always siding with the party most favourable to their ambitions and most convinced of their 'generosity'. The latter were usually the children least interested in family traditions and the land, the ones hankering after city pleasures, fine women, luxury and quick spending. Clever lawyers and professors from the law faculty in Recife hastened the ruin of the old planters and also swindled the state of millions in taxes by legally watertight manoeuvres. One of these lawyers became so famous that he soon left Brazil and worked for the vast empires of the New York monopolies; and so did many like him. The refinery-owners thus had two sure ways of making money: soaking the old landowners and evading taxes. Besides they were encouraged by the federal government.

A few plantation-owners who had inherited land back in the good old days of slavery now held out tooth and nail against the same tricks they had once used themselves to get rich. Most became cane growers for the refineries. The rest changed crops and let their land, and this also meant decline. The *casas grandes* were closing down because they were no longer the centre of economic, social and political life, and the owners were now finding out for themselves what it is to be a vassal. Most preferred to move to the near-by cities where they could educate their children without much hardship and try new kinds of economic activity.

Meanwhile the remaining woods were torn down and planted with cane, and this spoilt the soil. Erosion set in; land was repeatedly burnt off; rivers ran dry and rainfall became scarce. Nature was transformed, and so were the people living in the country.

The peasants I knew thirty years ago were not the same as the ones now joining the Peasant League. In those days their lands weren't accurately surveyed, nor were their fruit-gardens and other assets taxed. Many old planters struggled on in their new situation and sacrificed much of their property to educate their children; consequently their demands on their tenants hardened. Tenants' farms shrank and grew less fertile, and the tenants came trembling on rent day and went away in despair because all found their rents doubled or their lands reduced in size. Many gave up and went; but many more came back cap in hand to ask for another plot on even tougher terms.

A new figure now stood between master and tenants: the *administrador* or steward, normally a former peasant now employed as a rent-collector and tougher with his old workmates than the master himself. There were constant disputes over work or rent between *administradores* and labourers or tenant farmers, and some of the latter sought protection outside the estate by using their precious and hard-won voting rights which gave them influence with the local political boss. The local boss was normally a landowner or wealthy capitalist and usually held quantities of mortgage contracts and promissory notes; hence he could intervene with landowners to lower rents or stop farms being divided. But this was exceptional since few tenants had voting rights.

In general tenant farmers thirty to fifty years ago were more secure than the ones still surviving in the North-East. The population was less dense, there was more fertile land and the *latifundistas* were less ambitious and rapacious. This is not simply true of the North-East. Throughout the whole of Brazil and Latin America tenants' rights have suffered wherever new economic forces have conflicted with old in the struggle for land and labour.

CHAPTER 3

Passion and the North-East

From the first days of Portuguese colonization the North-East drew the attention of foreign and Brazilian writers – particularly the former – and their works are rich sources for social and economic historians. I too was later tempted by the idea of writing a history of the region and of following in the footsteps of such illustrious chroniclers as Gabriel Soares, Gandavo, Antonil, Koster, Saint Hilaire, Marcius, Lery, Rocha Pitta and a host of others. But such ideas had certainly never occurred to me when, at the age of thirteen, I and my brother were seated on our horses and led by father on a fine sorrel to Limoeiro, and then by car to Recife where we spent the next four years in a boarding-school.

At that time I was still totally under the influence of a wild childhood spent working and playing with the tenants' children: climbing trees to burn out wasps' nests with a brand in one hand and a sickle in the other, cutting cane for milling, galloping bareback across the fields and diving from the dikes. My first impulse on arrival was to run away, but no one would come with me and I spent the first year pacing up and down like a caged bird. I found it hard to adapt to my new life which I remember without pleasure. It was in that prison – which opened my mind to vast new possibilities – that I also discovered many kinds of evil and egoism. I've never been surprised by Raul Pompeia's descriptions of boarding-school life in his novel *The Atheneum,* and could add some more details were it my aim to portray some of the frustrated young men whose lives I had to share in that place. I was to meet many of them twenty years later as policemen, attorneys and even judges, taking out their frustrations on the people.

The headmaster was a law graduate embittered by the ruinous decline of his family who were landowners. He came from the lowlands of Paraíba, and underneath a veneer of culture he was basically a plantation foreman – a side of him always liable to burst out whenever he got into a rage. The boys, however, most of whom were from plantation-owners' families, were constantly tempted into trying his temper and provoked him till he exploded and insulted us, hit us about the head and kept us up all night. Anger eventually broke his heart and he died young.

A single anecdote will suffice to describe my life in that place. Whenever the breakfast bell rang at seven o'clock the boys would leap from their desks and charge towards the refectory door. The object of this Pavlovian reflex was to grab the best cup and lump of bread from the two long tables where we ate. But there were always three or four students left behind – including me – who would saunter casually to the refectory and have to make do with the smallest cup and the worst lump of dry, soggy or burnt bread. I was ashamed of causing trouble over such a trifle, but I couldn't tolerate this flagrant injustice and set myself to thinking up a plan which I put into practice methodically. Every morning I picked up two or three of the smallest cups and threw them into the backyard next door. When they found out there were only the big cups left, the head was informed; but since he had no way of discovering the saboteur, he ordered that the cups be replaced by even bigger ones and insisted that we should be served a special watery coffee. This put an end to the seven o'clock charge since no one cared whether he ate good or bad bread with such vile coffee. I consoled myself with the thought that we were at least getting equal treatment. Throughout I had been spurred by the same sense of justice which in later life propelled me out of normal society into the turmoils of social and political struggle.

Then came university. I wasn't a particularly hard-working student because I made up my mind when I entered the law faculty at Recife (I was then eighteen) to cut the ties to my father's purse strings. I managed to buy a small boys' school at a modest price, and took up primary teaching in Olinda, the old capital of Pernambuco. António Almeida came in as my partner and I shall never forget him: he died too young some years later when he was working as a doctor on a typhoid epidemic in the Paraíba *sertão*.

I had hoped to be a surgeon and ended up a law graduate because a poor student in a capitalist régime is obliged to work and cannot always choose the career that suits him. I'm sure today that had I been a doctor I would still have ended up in jail or exile like so many others, since I would still have come into contact with the problems which wedded my life to the peasants and eventually cost me everything, including the right to live in my own country. The number of lawyers who will defend peasants simply out of a sense of justice is pitifully small. On the other hand a growing number of doctors are going over to Marxism, socialism and communism as a result of their contact with poverty and misery; and if I had been a doctor – especially in the North-East – and had had to handle the skeletal bodies of those victims of the cane and cassava fields and the *cambão*, I would probably have rebelled even more violently against the system.

The festering sore of north-eastern social conditions has never been cured by palliatives and there is only one answer: radical surgery. There has never been a lack of powerful and eloquent voices to denounce the region's sick society with its poverty-stricken coastal fishermen and the *sertão* where religious fanatic and *cangaceiro** typify a permanent atmosphere of lawlessness and violence. Men like António Pedro de Figueredo, 'Cousin Fusco',† Brother Caneca the martyr of Brazilian radicalism, and Cipriano Barata‡ who spent many years in the country's worst jails for his ideas and intransigence – these are but a few of the nineteenth-century heroes who denounced the crimes of rich against poor. Nor did they merely denounce: they also took part in the risings in Pernambuco and Bahia which shook that selfish, feudal and slave-owning society to its core.

I have always tended to sympathize with men who go beyond mere words and throw their lot in with popular revolts because I believe that the humane and just attitude lies in sharing the masses' life and acting rather than simply shouting and denouncing.

From the remotest past there has been an unbroken tradition of protest by men who voiced the deepest aspirations of the poor and oppressed, especially in the Brazilian North-East and Pernambuco. I could list a hundred or more in every walk of life including politics, teaching, journalism, poetry, medicine, law, religion, economics or government – all closely linked with popular resistance and ready at the barricades in popular revolts to shed their blood in the common cause of the people. But to do this would be to yield to my erstwhile urge to be a historian, and if readers are curious about the past I refer them to the invaluable works of Professor Amaro Quintas or Mauro Mota, director of the Joaquim Nabuco Institute of Social Research in Recife. These two scholars

*Cangaceiro means bandit.

† A nineteenth-century half-caste revolutionary nicknamed 'Dark Cousin'. He was active in the 1848 rising in Recife.

‡ A revolutionary of the same period, much persecuted for his ideals.

will dispel any false ideas about the submissiveness of the Brazilian people which the reader may have formed from histories written by collaborators with the ruling classes in a country where the latter have always been composed predominantly of the most reactionary elements – the rich landowners.

The only social class to indulge in political dialogue in Brazil has been the ruling class itself which has usually contained two (and only two) fundamentally indistinguishable factions. For example the conservatives and liberals who supported the Second Empire of Pedro II* – one of the longest-lasting and most oppressive of the world's empires, based throughout its fifty years on African slavery and peasant serfdom.

The common people have never negotiated any kind of agreement with the status quo because they have always been discriminated against and excluded from the nation's political life, despite the fact that they are its mainstay. Such excursions as I made into Brazilian history – from the days of the anti-Dutch guerrilla wars led by Felipe Camarão till modern times – convinced me that the just cause is the cause of the people: who give everything and receive nothing, not even the right to work, security, education or freedom. And anyone who commits himself to such a cause must do so unconditionally: he either gives himself totally or ends up betraying the cause and capitulating to the enemy.

There is no need to turn to our contemporary Christian and non-Christian radicals in seeking to justify such a commitment. Brother Caneca, the north-eastern agitator, formulated it 150 years ago when he faced the firing-squad:

*Emperor of Brazil between 1841 and November 1889, when the republic was proclaimed. He was personally a liberal-minded man, no doubt more progressive than the society around him. He presided over Abolition in 1888.

'Whoever governs – noble or workman, rich or poor, wise or ignorant, black or white, brown or red – there is only one party: the party of civil liberty and the happiness of the people; and anything that opposes it must be fought with fire and steel.'

These were the motives which, with others I shall describe later, finally converted the shy planter's son and quiet student into a social agitator. I say social agitator with pride because it is an honourable name and I utter it out of patriotism with no thought of personal gain, patronage, glory or gratitude. But I have found peace of conscience since I have offered myself in an unflinching effort to follow in the steps of the revolutionaries of Minas Gerais and 1817, and of the abolitionists of 1888, and throughout, my thoughts have been fixed firmly on the people, my country and the future. I have been an agitator. Life is inconceivable without agitation. Agitation is like the wind that carries pollen to the flowers or the flow of blood through a body. Without these, life stagnates and dies; and to reject agitation is to refuse unrest and movement and to deny the laws of nature, science and justice. The crime lies in refusing to agitate: in stagnating. A society without agitation and unrest is like a fetid pool and its institutions languish and decay. This is why one can never suppress agitation, and why it is absurd to condemn it: because agitation and movement are permanent features of life whatever the epoch or circumstances. Because agitation is caused by the passion for truth.

*

On 16 December 1939 I graduated with 119 others from the country's oldest and most famous law school. Nearly all my fellow students were sons of north-eastern landowners, and this was in conformity with a tradition dating from centuries ago when rich ranchers, plantation-owners and traders sent their cleverest and least rurally-inclined sons back to

Portugal to study at Coimbra and return with a diploma in Latin stamped with the royal seal.

Despite the War, which was about to inflame Europe and the world and alter human history, all of us who graduated that year came down the steps from the old law school with our minds firmly fixed on nothing but our future careers.

At that time Brazil was under the dictatorship of Getulio Vargas which lasted till the end of the War in 1945. But despite everything the civil courts were functioning normally, and in the year I graduated a law was passed simplifying and unifying commercial and civil legal procedure throughout the whole federation. Many of my fellow students already had their careers mapped out. Some were counting on the fat sinecures usually reserved by banks, factories and companies for sons of their own members or best customers. Others already had places as appeal judges or were preparing for seats in the high court. A few – the ones full of theories and superstitious awe for bourgeois legal institutions, notably the sanctity of property – were continuing their studies to write theses and take up lectureships or even chairs. And many simply went on sporting a well-trimmed moustache, polished nails and the latest fashion in suits and shoes so as to show off their graduate's rings made of fine carat gold set with a shining, polished ruby and real diamonds. Thus equipped they waited for a good match: a girl from high society was a better catch than a professorial chair, a cushy job or a post as legal adviser in a bank or refinery office. Finally there were some who had political ambitions and had, with their family's help, arranged for themselves to be elected with the return of democracy. During those years of Vargas's dictatorship democracy – in the words of Agamemnon Magalhães – was a withered stick, just as it is now under the military dictatorship.

There were few left unwilling to let themselves be caught

in the golden web of a system which was still in force despite popular revolts and civil wars. I was among them.

The examination in political and social theory created much debate in the corridors of the law faculty and gave rise to the formation of irreconcilable factions and parties. The dictatorship was careful to prevent this debate from spreading, and rigidly controlled the circulation of ideas in the country by means of the infamous D.I.P. or Department of Press and Propaganda. In Pernambuco the political police were specially vigilant with the students, and only a distant and muffled echo of our polemics ever filtered down to the people outside. There were two well-defined groups: the Right led by the *integralistas* or 'greenshirts' or 'green chickens' as we called them; and the Left headed by supporters of the communist Luiz Carlos Prestes and other revolutionary groups. Between them stood a group of neutrals and the mass of apathetic spectators who were always trying to patch up some compromise position or agreement between the two hostile camps.

When I arrived at the school at the age of eighteen I was already a left-winger and had begun to read Marx, but I was still not sure that this had put me on the road which would eventually lead me to an understanding of my fellow men.

Two years before I graduated I was jailed for the first time. A friend of mine who had become a student orator sent me a long letter from another city where he was on holiday. It was a passionate defence of Marx written with his usual enthusiasm and intelligence, and it fell into the hands of the political police. My house was ransacked and my modest library rifled, and I was led by two policemen to the presence of the Chief of Social and Political Order who was a graduate from the same law faculty. It would be an idea to investigate the role of some of the products of that school, many of whom have later become notorious as torturers of political prisoners; or grown so rich from gambling, extortion and prostitution rackets that they have ended up in the Chamber of Deputies or as rich appeal judges or attorneys. I suppose my first spell in prison – which only lasted twenty-four hours – was really a baptism by fire, a foretaste of what was to come.

The certain thing is that as I came down the faculty steps with my degree a few days after attending the graduation speech by Soriano Neto – the students' idol in those years – I had my mind made up: I would be a lawyer. But I still had to decide whether to defend the bankers and *latifundistas* or their employees, a decision which did not take long.

This was not a question of sectarianism, but of principle and political logic. I decided to support the cause of the poor and oppressed; and with this resolution firmly in mind I made my way to the High Court, a squat, ornate building one always approached from the sides since the back entrance was always barred and the front, with its vast stone steps and hideous façade, repelled entry rather than invited it.

Pernambuco High Court will testify that in my twenty years there as a lawyer my decision to defend the poor and oppressed not only brought me no personal wealth but won me a great deal of hatred and prejudice from influential circles. For I never limited myself to defending such meagre rights as the poor possess: I also took every opportunity during pleas and appeals to denounce the evil social institutions I saw around me. The usual image of lawmen talking blissfully of justice and law has nothing in common with the undignified spectacle – the back-stabbing, manoeuvres and chicanery – one sees in and out of court when certain unlawful or even criminal interests come under attack. A case never had any value or interest save as a possible source of fees: one lawyer, one of the cleverest and most formidable I ever encountered, had written an immense tome about the role of the lawyer – his ethics, place in history, and relationships with judiciary and clients – and was much admired by his pupils. However when it came to actual cases he was not only completely unprincipled in his methods against his opponents, he also defended himself against his own clients: demanding not only a contract for payment of fees with all the necessary legal guarantees but also a blank cheque which he locked in his safe and cashed ruthlessly and swiftly at a suitable moment. He was one of the more respectable, and one can picture the terrible disillusion of young graduates when they eventually faced their former teachers across the courtroom and discovered the idol had feet of clay.

I and many of my colleagues were therefore understandably moved one evening to see Clovis Bevilaqua making his last visit before his death to the law faculty at Recife. Bevilaqua was the faculty's greatest teacher, and his project for a Brazilian civil code was undoubtedly a valuable work within the limits of bourgeois jurisprudence. After a century of dispute and conflict it finally came into effect on the eve of the Russian October Revolution – which was to throw out bourgeois law completely and install a new proletarian legality, and also radically subvert the political, economic and social order which had hitherto prevailed in the world. Bevilaqua died old and penniless. But unlike some jurists of his stature – for example Rui Barbosa or Epitácio Pessoa – there was nothing, not even an anecdote, to compromise his memory in the minds of his pupils and opponents, with whom he did battle with scrupulous fairness and honesty.

The years that followed were ones of intense activity for me as a lawyer and revealed more of the difficulties and pitfalls which the legal profession holds for a person who adopts my sort of political philosophy. I was unyielding in defence of my principles; but at every step I met obstacles not only within the law itself but in the attitudes of the judges who defended the system perpetuated by the social class in whose service they were consciously working. Consequently I was fighting on more than one front and preferred to lose on points rather than abandon principles.

In a society where judges move in capitalist circles and serve capitalist interests the laws they apply are themselves simply a reflection of those interests. History will condemn them as it has done so many times before. It was the judges and not the people who dictated the monstrous sentence against Tiradentes and his descendants in succeeding generations. They even sentenced his house to be demolished and the site ploughed up with salt so that grass wouldn't grow there. It is also the judges, not the people, who apply what they call sacrosanct and immutable legal norms to evict peasants from the land they live on, thus contradicting a principle which must one day apply to all judges: land belongs to the man who works it and inhabits it.

I shall mention later some concrete examples of the judges' methods which are doubtless logical in terms of their principles. Let me for the moment speak of those magistrates who despite everything struggle valiantly to defend the oppressed and the victims of injustice, and strive to attenuate the law and speak out in their sentences against the obstacles to justice, human understanding and equality. Such judges, unlike the overwhelming majority of their colleagues, have understood the conflict between life and law because they have seen that law should be designed to serve life and not vice versa.

When law no longer applies to the majority or totality of a society it becomes oppressive, a refuge for a group, caste or minority bent on halting the society's development and stifling its vital energy. It must then be reformed or abolished. But how can this be done? It seems impossible to achieve a situation where the peasantry would have a right to the peaceful and permanent possession of the land they cultivate if they are never to get the means of buying it in the first place. And how can there be any progress if failure to pay rents of a third or a half of their produce – or *cambão*, or extras for a horse, cow or goat – constitutes in the eyes of the minority an act of violence against the laws and customs of the society? Any refusal to observe these feudal practices is considered an attack on the prevailing order and a crime against the security of the state; and it was this sort of consideration which conditioned my decision to abandon law and take up political agitation.

In dialectical terms I underwent a 'change of quality'; but it wasn't enough. Even when I had a political platform from which to denounce the victimization of the oppressed, my words fell on the deaf ears of audiences composed mostly of rich land- and refinery-owners, planters, cane-producers, ranchers and their staunchest supporters like bankers, businessmen and their legal advisers. The press and the spoken word were controlled by these economic forces, and my protests were distorted and minimized. They also controlled the apparatus of political repression as well as most of the judges and propaganda outlets. They could also count on the backwardness of the rural masses who for centuries have been isolated and disorganized, and who were being herded by parish priests into the harmless refuge of a church which had no interest in their problems.

I realized I was at the foot of a difficult mountain where on every path an ambush lay concealed; but I didn't hesitate over the choice between populist demagoguery and revolutionary radicalism. I chose the mountain because I'm the sort of man for whom danger is always outweighed by the prospect of new horizons. Moreover I had acquired enough experience over the years not to be deterred by setbacks and hardships. I stuck to it even when I was abandoned by friends who had started out with me; and even when I was

Passion and the North-East 45

later faced with envy, treachery and cowardice in my most difficult moments.

Even among those who clearly understood the people's problems and the need for a profound social revolution, there were many who opposed immediate action and counselled apathy for fear of haste and unnecessary bloodshed. I answered them by pointing out that if the revolutions of this century of popular revolt had been conducted in accord with the advice of moderate and timorous men, not a single one would have achieved its goals. No man is indispensable; and revolutions triumph, as Lenin said, where popular energies flow fastest. But these energies have to be created. They are not generated spontaneously as some cosy optimists maintain : they are created by men who love the people and whose thoughts are focused on reality. In other words by the revolutionaries.

PART TWO

Encounter with the Peasant

CHAPTER 1

The Peasant and Humanity

Each of us has a peasant within us. Whether one lives in New York, Paris or London and has never been to the countryside, one feels a sudden sadness on looking from an apartment window and glimpsing a solitary tree against the monotony of a city or the crude outline of the skyscrapers. The tree evokes ancestors who were peasants, and the sight of it fills one with a sense of exile; for we have all come from the countryside, whether we are the rich in search of more wealth or the poor looking for a new life. A tree amongst the cement and concrete can wake a sudden memory of fields left behind in a shadowy past. We can forget childhood, love, sorrow or joy; we can forget all these intangible things but we always remember the land, even when it is no longer under our feet or we are not sitting in the shade of a tree. The soil is stronger than our blood; it flows in it and feeds it; it is life itself. That is why a solitary tree can stimulate a longing for the land we have lost.

Man is basically the land he lives on. Every furrow he ploughs is an act of hope, every seed sown a gesture of love, and every harvest a hymn of triumph. It has always been thus; but there is a difference between man's being part of the earth and the degrading greed which makes him take it for his private property when it should be the centre and sustenance of all mankind. Gerrard Winstanley, the English seventeenth-century mystic, was quick to point out that throughout history civil war and revolution have originated essentially from social divisions resting on the private possession of land: 'Private property not only divided society into rich and poor, but dehumanized the rich and degraded the poor.' Men have spilt rivers of blood and raised mountains of corpses for the possession of land; but since the first cave drawings the creations of human genius have been inspired by the soil and its fruits more than by any other of man's prized possessions. There is no religious sect, sacred text or code of laws, nothing that reflects human aspirations or limitations which does not reveal the permanent and intimate union of man and the earth. Yet although the earth is his mother, man is an errant child: he kills to possess her for himself, and this is his tragedy – a tragedy that can only be avoided by creating a new kind of man free from avarice, selfishness and the urge to dominate the land for himself.

Throughout the history of human civilization the peasant has always borne the heaviest burden. It is no exaggeration to say that for thousands of years the peasant has occupied the middle ground between beast of burden and landowner; and since he is treated like an ox or horse he is really more like an animal than a man, in terms of the quantity of his labours and his primitive life. Whether as a serf, slave, hired labourer or tenant farmer, we find him doing the hardest tasks, and nearly always without much hope of reward. Day and night, year after year, he is bent over the soil, and he organizes his life round the movements of the sun and stars and passing seasons; for life itself depends on a good harvest.

Since he must live his whole life on the land, the peasant's consciousness is moulded to a conception of the world and a system of ideas and reactions which is virtually impenetrable to the outsider. The peasant has his own philosophy which is radically different from that of the city dweller, and distinct

The Peasant and Humanity 51

even from that of his brother and natural ally, the urban proletarian.

His mind works differently from the latter's, even though both expend similar amounts of energy in creating other people's wealth. The peasant understands the moon which shines on his fields and fiestas, fills his imagination with dreams and his songs with love and nostalgia, and tells him when he must sow his crops. He rises at daybreak, and sunset is his signal to down his tools and make his tired way home, his heart lightened by the hope of a good harvest if his land is his own; humiliated and melancholy if he works for a master. The stars are his silent guides: he tries to puzzle out their meaning and gives them affectionate names like 'The Three Marias' or 'Papa Ceia' – but he must never point his finger at them or his body will be covered with warts. He crosses himself and mutters 'God bring you to the sea' whenever he sees a silver shooting star flare on a clear night. 'Santiago's Way'* is his horoscope and helps him forecast sun or rain; and so do the length or colour of a sunset, rings round the moon, lightning in the north, and the songs of certain birds on summer nights. His senses grow immensely sharp, especially his sight and hearing: eyes which continually scan the horizon for stars seem to find their proper element in the pure infinite light of nature. Looking down he sees the earth and new furrows, the fresh seed or the falling corn, and at evening he can watch the colours of the sunset, the stars and the birth or death of the moon. He goes to bed early.

Euclides da Cunha and Sarmiento, authors of brilliant studies of the *sertão* peasants and the Argentinian *gaucho*, marvel at the ability of peasant trackers to follow a man or beast through forests or thick undergrowth, summer or winter, over periods of days and many miles until they finally

---

*The Milky Way.

discover their victim's hiding place. This extraordinary ability of the peasant would put a Sherlock Holmes to shame. Their sharp eyes can pick out the smallest traces left by a passing man or beast, for they can quickly spot where a twig or stone has been kicked over leaving its damp side exposed to the sun. The famous north-east *cangaceiros* António Silvino and Virgulino Lampião were both skilful trackers. One of their tricks for confusing the police and throwing them off the trail was to put their sandals on backwards so as to send their pursuers in the wrong direction.

But if the peasant's eyes are always filled with the light of the sky and stars, his ears too are accustomed to silence. Silence is his constant companion and teacher: from it he learns to pick out the faintest sounds and tell one from another. His ears grow sensitive with listening to the leaves and murmuring waters, to the call of birds, sheep and oxen and the tinkle of herd bells. These things train his hearing to the subtler sounds of the night so that when he is walking in the dark he can tell you what animals he has startled along his path, and can tell without looking whether an approaching horse belongs to a friend or stranger. When he's hunting he can calculate the direction and distance of his prey from his hiding place in the bushes simply by sound.

In all this he is quite unlike the city dweller whose sight is bounded by streets and high buildings, neon lights, books, television, and films; and whose ears are constantly subjected to sudden and violent noises. With his senses sharpened by nature the peasant is capable of feats undreamed of by town dwellers. He can perform marvels as a tracker, herder, hunter or guerrilla fighter, and many a fine book has been written to tell of his skills. Such books also tell that the finest contributions and sacrifices in the revolutions and civil wars of history have been made by the peasant. This is natural, because the peasant is the quintessence of humanity.

The Peasant and Humanity

The peasant is shaped by his environment, by his backwardness, by the kind of work he must do, by his contact generation after generation with the earth, and by the traditions of a life where every father is a model for his son and every uncle for his nephew in a monotonous chain of lives all sharing the same beginning and end.

This stable existence gives each peasant a physiognomy and character which make him seem at first sight indistinguishable from the next. Such a way of life gives the peasant a firm and settled vision of the world, and any encounter with him is difficult if one tries to challenge his preconceptions. It is impossible to win his confidence if one confronts his world head-on. It is mistaken to treat him like a factory-worker, student or intellectual, because the latter live in very different conditions. A follower of Freud will be disappointed to find no trace of pederasty among the peasantry; but an orthodox Marxist will also be disillusioned by the difficulty he will experience in adjusting to the peasant's idea of himself.

It is not enough to reflect on the peasant's lot and think up the correct way of liberating him. One has to live with him and share his existence; and one must learn to accept him as he is, with all his individualism, impulsiveness and mysticism. There is no other way of winning his support. I speak from experience; because a lifetime spent with the peasants – first as a child and later as a revolutionary – has taught me how to approach him, and what language to use to bring him out of his shell into bolder and more effective attitudes.

The peasant thinks differently from the factory-worker because, isolated with his wife and children, his thoughts are constantly turned to the land which absorbs all his energies and shapes the course of his life. If the land belongs to him he will fight desperately to keep it, and if it belongs to another he will constantly cherish the hope of possessing it some day. A peasant's land is his life; but the factory-worker must work alongside scores or hundreds of workmates whose situation is identical to his own. Consequently the factory itself does not dominate his thoughts: his concern is with wages and other issues like working hours, holidays, security and housing. He must turn constantly to his fellow workers, whose support and solidarity he needs, to protect rights won in a common struggle. He realizes he cannot strike on his own, so the factory-worker is necessarily a collectivist who, when he is struggling for money, is consciously aware that he is not out for merely personal gain. In this way the urban worker loses a sense of his own individuality and is integrated into the community of his workmates. His world is essentially distinct from that of the peasant, and in each case different conditions generate a different psychology.

The peasant is closer to the craftsman because both have control over the means of production – in the case of the peasant, the land; and this makes him an individualist, unlike the factory-worker who has no control over the instruments and fruits of his labour. This is why it is mistaken to attempt unthinkingly to transplant to peasant life work methods which have succeeded with the proletariat, without a previous and sustained campaign of political education.

The peasant's individualism makes him suspicious and withdrawn; and such individualism will not be overcome by the superficial contact attempted during the 'revolutionary weekends' in vogue with certain young, romantic and sectarian students – even if the latters' intentions are honourable. One must live with the peasant and share his world. It then becomes clear that he is not simply an individualist but is also fundamentally impulsive in his attitudes due to the isolated and insecure life he leads at the mercy of harvest and landowner. His individualism and impulsiveness will push him to extremes and he can go from submission to revolt in an instant.

The Peasant and Humanity

Oppressed and bound to the land, the peasant is like a stick of dynamite waiting for a fuse. But it's no simple thing to get the charge to explode: it needs patience, and the peasant's mistrust and shyness won't succumb to mere words. If words are not followed up with action he stays withdrawn and goes on waiting, just as he will wait for the sun or rain or harvest. In the meantime he dreams of his land and liberty because, caught in the pincer-like grip of an insensitive society, he transfers his deepest aspirations to a dream-world and waits for a miracle.

Meanwhile he goes on working the land for little or nothing, because the land is his stomach and his life. And freedom is like the wind in the trees: he can feel the land under his feet and strike it with his hoe; it is the blood in his veins, flesh of his flesh. But freedom is like the wind he cannot touch but which he knows exists; and he communicates with God through these two symbols of land and wind. He suffers for the land as though he were sacrificing himself for his God; and he waits for liberty, which will be his resurrection and second life.

Together these two ideals, land and liberty, signify peace and an end to suffering and humiliation; and this is the root of his submissiveness and Christianity – his almost Buddhist Catholicism. This is no abstract or pure faith, but rather a blend of real and unreal, of God and the World, of land and liberty, which gives rise to his mysticism. But until the day when land and liberty are joined and the symbols of his mysticism are united, he will go on letting himself be led like a sleepwalker down the same paths towards his own sacrifice. A few may rebel on the way, fight, achieve epic fame, and then be isolated and destroyed. Sometimes a large group will form and for a time do heroic and irrelevant things which lead nowhere. But the immense masses of sacrificial victims go on waiting and retelling the legends and songs which are their life-blood. ... The rebels are the lightning in the north announcing a coming storm. Their finest symbol is Lampião, the greatest of the *cangaceiros*.

But if it is not the *cangaceiros*, it is the *beatos*: religious preachers or visionaries who fill their lives with hopes and fears through their imprecations against the world and their muddled fanaticism and promises which – like the *cangaceiros'* – lead nowhere. The prototype of such religious men was O *Conselheiro*.* Such phenomena come and go in the North-East in cycles like an intermittent fever, and usually coincide with the periods of drought which are not so much their cause as their immediate impulse. They are caused by the misery of the *latifundio* and are not merely accidental phenomena; they are more like sudden torrents bursting out of the earth and devastating the land and then sinking back underground leaving a strange muffled sound behind. It is easy to understand why the peasants exalt both *beato* and *cangaceiro* simultaneously because the former always announces the end of the world in an apocalypse of fire, and the latter is the avenging warrior who will destroy the oppressive world with his knife and gun.

When the peasant manages to shake off his inertia he is capable of destroying himself for one or other of these figures and his faith will become paroxysmal and frantic. Since the *cangaceiro* and *beato* are similar in many ways it's not hard to believe in both; and if either is killed this simply adds to the peasant's rage and frustration.

But faith channels this frustration into hopes for resurrection. According to the simplest and most desperate peasants the bandit Lampião didn't die but was called by Father Cícero

* 'The Counsellor' António Maciel, leader of a messianic movement against the 'atheists' republic' which aimed to found a north-eastern theocracy. He and his peasant followers held out in Bahia for three years until 1899.

The Peasant and Humanity 57

do Juàzeiro;* and the enormous mass of peasants believes that Father Cícero will one day come back. The basis of such sublime and nonsensical belief is a yearning for revenge and justice, and the phenomenon is universal wherever conditions exist for it to emerge.

*Juàzeiro is a town about 330 miles from the capital of Ceara. Father Cícero convinced many peasants of his miraculous powers, and eventually became vice-president of the state. Pilgrimages to his old hermitage are still common. He died in 1934.

CHAPTER 2

Religion, *Cachaça, Capanga*

I said that the peasant is like dynamite waiting for a match and a fuse, but that these are not easy to supply although the operation may seem simple. The reason is that the person who makes the dynamite – the *latifundista* – also has many effective and carefully-calculated ways of stopping match and fuse from contacting the charge.

One way is religion. Marx's famous statement about religion being the opium of the people is exactly applicable to the landless, enslaved peasantry. Basically every religion seeks to save man and elevate him so that he may be deserving of God's grace and eternal life. But the supreme obstacle to such ideals is always man himself, because he can never escape reality and the conditions which bind him to the world and shape his life and outlook.

Christianity was the religion of the oppressed peoples of Judea and the slaves of Rome, but in the Middle Ages it was deformed and absorbed by the feudal state to become an instrument in the hands of oppressive feudal barons. Wars were and still are waged for Christianity. It decked itself out with banners and coats of arms in the Crusades and marshalled soldiers and weapons. Under the Inquisition it murdered and humiliated in the same way that Christ its founder was murdered and humiliated. Such resistance as was offered by the few men with the vocation to defend and propagate its true principles was exceptional.

Religion, Cachaça, Capanga

The peasantry of the West accepted Christianity exactly as it was presented to them over the generations: as a belief capable of saving them from original sin and hell-fire provided that they kept absolute and blind obedience to God, church, barons and authorities. Despite this revolts against the oppressors broke out and were put down by fire and sword. The peasant wars of eastern Europe in the fifteenth and sixteenth centuries demonstrate the scale of these rebellions and the severity with which they were repressed.

The curious thing is that these revolts against hunger and the peasant's burden of labour and taxation were seemingly justified by appeals to Christianity itself; and that religions – especially the Christian religion whose principles are one of humanity's finest legacies – are capable of inspiring rebellion among the victims of injustice. The oppressors know this but have much more experience than the oppressed; and they defend themselves using a religious faith which should have belonged to the poor but was usurped by the rich.

Despite the example of some extraordinary figures like John Huss, Bartolomé de las Casas and Frei Caneca, the church did all it could to slow and halt the progress of the peasantry towards their goal of land and liberty, and thus sided with the ruling classes of the day. It did even worse when it sanctioned repression, violence and war in the name of immutable dogmas. As Winstanley states:

Government was established and maintained to protect the interests of property owners; and organized religion arose to inspire the poor to submission by attributing the social order to Divine Providence. Since the social order was conceived and maintained in the interests of the wealthy, it was logical that they and their representatives in the church could not tolerate the destruction of that system.

This painful truth enunciated by Winstanley three centuries ago is still embedded like a thorn deep in the heart of the peasantry. Such heroic and tenacious attempts as were made by a few priests to raise oppressed against oppressors have been denounced as treachery and madness and punished savagely. And then paradoxically these heroic martyrs have in turn been used as an opiate to dull any new signs of the rebelliousness which springs up when stomachs are empty. The peasant adopts a mystical attitude to these pure and ingenuous priest-victims, and sees their rebellion as a projection of his own revolt and sacrifice; and this comforts him and sends him back to sleep.

Another non-violent way of making the peasant sleep is cheap rum. From the first days of colonization its use became general in Brazil despite sanctions by the authorities who actually prohibited its manufacture lest it hinder sugar production. At first rum was produced on a small scale with make-shift equipment and it used up cane which wealthy plantation-owners would rather have turned into sugar. But as soon as the masters saw that rum was in general use and therefore easily marketable, they started setting aside a portion of their cane crop for distilling; and in some cases rum raised more money than sugar itself. Soon the previously reluctant owners were investing in copper stills; and eventually one rarely saw a plantation where sugar and rum production were not carried on simultaneously. A number also devoted themselves exclusively to *cachaça*, the name given to cane rum by the north-easterners; and during the big slumps when a load of sugar wouldn't even cover its own freight charges, the cane was used for alcohol and the cleverest growers thus avoided financial ruin.

Sugar is basically noble because – especially when white or refined – it is rarely seen in a peasant's house, whereas *cachaça* abounds. The peasant needs it as a drug to go on living; and because of it he dies young or forgoes what little freedom he has as well as losing his reason; or is degraded completely. ... The hospitals, alms-houses and jails receive a growing number of victims every year and statistics are soaring alarmingly. *Cachaça* itself is also going downhill. At first it was carefully distilled in clay or copper pots and exported. But standards were later lowered when large-scale consumption demanded increased quantities. Recently it has become practice to mix *cachaça* with certain noxious chemicals and to sell it faster under attractive brand-names. The chosen victim is usually the peasant who needs the poisonous drug to forget life and escape into his world of dreams. Basically he uses it to cheat hunger.

While *cachaça* can make a material fortune for wholesalers and retailers, it can also give the peasant a fleeting illusion of wealth, freedom and power. He breakfasts on a mouthful of rum, and rum is waiting on his master's fields to cheer him and degrade him. ... Since the rich also get drunk, the peasant justifies himself with anecdotes and rhymes passed from mouth to mouth; for example:

> Once it used to be
> The blacks and browns who drank;
> And now even noble men
> Are tipsy every day.
> I've even seen Your Worship
> Falling on his face.
> It's not a sin to drink
> When you enjoy God's grace.

The alcoholic wretch is drawn irresistibly by the smell when he opens the bottle, and drinks the foaming, crystalline *cachaça* in a single gulp which illuminates his face as no piece of meat will ever do – if ever he's lucky enough to get meat. *Cachaça* goes with him everywhere and dominates his behaviour in a way that belief in God never does; for the peasant says: '*Cachaça*'s more mighty than God, for God proposes and *cachaça* disposes.' The authorities try to stamp the substance out not because of the evil and devastation it causes, but because of all goods it is the one which evades most taxes. The distillers sell it tax-free, and the retailer – the 'rum-man' – also pays no tax thanks to a complicated series of stratagems based on collaboration between all parties from producer to alcoholic. *Cachaça* is a criminal and outlaw from the moment it drips from the tubes of the still, already impregnated with lead salts, to the time it adds to the degradation and demoralization of the addict. Liquor is so intimately bound up with the existence of the *latifundio* that the day the bond is broken the latter will be shaken to its foundations. One can understand why the peasant needs to drown his cares in *cachaça*; but it remains unforgivable. *Cachaça* becomes his second nature and under its influence he can be led docilely by anyone who cares to exploit him, because it deprives the peasant of all his moral energy and rebellion and resigns him to his hoeing and digging without protest. He gives himself body and soul to *cachaça* as if it were his God.

Such are the pacific and subtle means whereby the peasant is dominated, tamed and kept in a permanent state of intoxication where he cannot even use his reason. But there are also other, violent means, such as the *capanga*, or hired thug, and the armed police. The *capanga* is the law inside the *latifundio* and the policeman represents law in the outside world. To escape from one is to fall into the clutches of the other. The police and army are merely hired killers in disguise who lie in wait for the peasant when he leaves the confines of the *latifundio* and goes to town on market, festival or churchdays. He fears the military more than the *capanga* because the latter is a peasant like himself who is also liable to lose his land and the privileges which allow him to carry a gun and do his master's bidding. The military is more powerful because the police or army can disarm a *capanga*, arrest and shoot him as part of their duties 'in legitimate defence of the social order'. Behind the military stand the police chiefs and judges who represent order, security and property.

Since the peasant will never have to call on these figures to defend rights he doesn't possess, they only affect other people and the peasant remains a passive outsider. But in the name of such shadowy entities the soldier can draw his pistol or knife or slide his carbine from his knapsack or saddle-bags and lay down the law in the middle of the street, or in a fair or festival; and no man dares utter a word or gesture of protest. But the peasant is like a charge waiting for a fuse; and when the moment comes he will go from one extreme to the other, and all the religions, *cachaça*, *capangas*, soldiers, laws and restrictions in the world won't stop him.

CHAPTER 3

The Peasant of the North-East

From the first century after the discovery of Brazil ambitions for wealth and power combined to create more massive concentrations of black African slaves in the North-East than in other parts of the country, this phenomenon being due to the existence in the region of a dark, fertile clay called *massapê*, and to the versatility and quick growth of the sugar cane.

Sweet to the masters, bitter to the slaves, sugar determined the future of both. Out of this new society based on the co-existence – or rather juxtaposition – of black slaves and their masters, arose a colourful language whose symbolism was blended from religion and sensuality, animism, mythology and aphrodisiac magic. This language gave the popular poetry of the region an enormous power and none of its great scholars or poets has entirely escaped its influence: even sociologists and politicians draw on its rich imagery full of the bitterness and irony of suffering.

The geography of the North-East is by now well known due to the attention given to it by the international press, especially the press of the United States. It consists of three regions: the *mata*, or green coastal belt; the *agreste*, a barren, rocky region; and the *sertão*, the wild hinterland. Actually there is a fourth region between the *mata* and *agreste*, an intermediate zone combining aspects of both. The wild *sertão* offers a hard living for ranchers and cotton-growers, and the *mata* is given over entirely to cane-growing. Between them the *agreste* is divided up predominantly between middle and small property-owners who grow cereals of various kinds.

The three zones form a system of intercommunication where the *sertão* provides cattle and cotton for the *mata* which sends sugar, *rapadura*,* *cachaça*, cloth and fruit back up to the *sertão*; while the *agreste* provides flour, maize and beans as well as other produce also to be found in the other regions. Since the *mata* is the most fertile region and best irrigated by rainfall and waterways, it contains the densest population and the most *latifundios*. In this region hired labourers and tenant farmers abound, lorded over by refinery-owners and absentee landlords. The refinery-owners can count on cheap and plentiful labour, and the landlords put up the rents and demand various other sorts of payment.

Small tenant farmers and *minifundio* owners move down from the *agreste* to the *mata* and thus add to the region's growing poverty problem. And then, during bad droughts when they have no alternative, the inhabitants of the *sertão* come down too. The peasants from the *agreste* zone, however, only stay long enough to pay off their rent arrears or to give their over-farmed *minifundios* a fallow period; and the *sertanejo* merely awaits the first rains in the highlands. He always goes back and no one could ever stop him: he came down reluctantly, driven by the drought, and returns happily to rediscover his land, wet and covered with flowering ombu-trees and fattened goats and to find his old reliable donkeys. His descent was a temporary escape.

Since the opening of the new communications links with the South and the news of 'easy work' in the factories of São Paulo and the coffee plantations, the number of peasants coming down to the *mata* from the other two regions has been

*Rough, brown cane sugar eaten by the poor.

diminishing yearly. The migratory movement which was first from east to west and vice-versa and then northwards during the rubber boom, nowadays goes from north to south. This migration has been so intense that it has given rise to the invention of a sort of peasant transport called the *pau de arará*.

The inhabitant of the coastal belt or *mata* who is called *brejeiro*, and whom Euclides da Cunha describes as the 'neurasthenic coastal half-caste', also makes migratory trips, short tragic ones from the cane plantations to the coastal cities. He goes in fact even further, because he makes a visit to the nearest forest and cuts himself wood from the *apeiba* trees to make a *jangada* or fishing-raft of trunks lashed together. Then he hoists a sail, takes up his creels, nets and hooks and makes his perilous way out to sea to lead a sort of amphibious existence, taking cassava from the land and fish from the water, a mixture of which, spiced with chili and accompanied by a draught of *cachaça*, forms his staple diet. Then he gets drunk and dreams. The sea sounds like the wind in the cane fields, and the pennants on his raft are the green of the cane leaves and the white of the sea spray.

There is only one problem however. Whether he is a peasant in the cane fields or a fisherman he cannot improve his life. In a hovel in Recife on the edge of a stagnant mango-swamp life is worse. There he sinks slowly into the mud and the rest of his hopes die. The Promised Land turns out to be nothing more than a hell of mud and slime where the crabs, mussels and razor-clams of better days are growing scarce.

The north-eastern peasant is the most unstable element in the country because of the desperate shortage of land, the oppressive *latifundio* system and the droughts. He lives anywhere, but wherever he goes he carries his vision of the world, his vitality, initiative and courage. One must think of him as looking on the world from the point of an angle. Each side of the angle has a special symbolic significance in terms of his hopes and ambitions: land, for example, is associated with freedom; water with abundance and fertility; horses with markets and trading, and so on. Since the land creates all else it remains the centre, the turning point; because life is for him inconceivable without land, but land is unattainable without liberty; and consequently he flees dreaming of his land and searching for freedom. Uselessly. Everywhere the system is the same or worse. On the rubber plantations in the Amazon region; on the rice-paddies round São Francisco; on the coffee plantations in Paraná – it is always the same. A few make their way back but the majority can never return because they have sold up everything before their departure and taken all their belongings with them. So the majority despair.

However, the braver ones resist and fight back: we shall find them in Goiás, Mato-Grosso, São Paulo, Paraná – leaders with guns in their hands, fighting back against the *grileiros** and police, killing and being killed. They have their own uniform and a special silent language; for when they communicate they do so by symbols and images and if you want to get them out of this dumbness caused by centuries of oppression you must understand this symbolic language and reshape it. It has to be learnt and used if one is to talk back to them but refashioned into an organized and coherent language with clear meanings and objectives. This is the task of political indoctrination. Since the number of words the peasant uses to communicate with his world is as limited as his movements, resources and ambitions themselves, the political leader must eventually use his own language which is poor in expressions but rich in the quality of experiences it refers to.

This is what I did in the shape of primers or first readers

*See below, page 81.

circulated first in the North-East, then in the rest of Brazil and finally throughout the whole of Latin America. Success is not due to me, just as I never claim the glory of having founded the Peasants' League. It was the peasants themselves who did this, as can be seen in the history of their existence over the centuries everywhere. Its success belongs to each individual, anonymous peasant, each one gifted in discovering the true meaning of things in images wrought by long years and the wisdom of the people.

CHAPTER 4

An Ideological Word

Brazil has a peasant population numbering about fifty million, of whom no less than seventeen million are scattered throughout the North-East, especially in the humid coast zone and the semi-arid *agreste*. Of these seventeen million some fifteen million live by labouring, tied to the *latifundio* like slaves sentenced to life in the galleys. This immense mass is divided into proletariat, semi-proletariat and peasants. The first two categories include the hired labourers, squatters and *peões*.* The peasants† include the *foreiros* (tenant farmers), herdsmen, *parceiros*‡ and *posseiros*.§

It would be no exaggeration to say that virtually all these fifty million Brazilians live at starvation level in conditions of servitude under the *cambão* system and that their only escape from this tragic scheme is into outlawry, shanty-town life, vagabondage, prostitution, poorhouses, jail or ultimately death. They know nothing of kindergartens, schools, culture, good health, tranquillity; of anything in short which constitutes a decent life.

I must now speak of the peasants who were the mainstay

* *Peões*: plural for *peão* or landless peasant.

† Julião uses the word *camponês* (peasant) throughout to refer to the group which created the Peasant League, i.e. tenants and others as opposed to hired labourers with whom he is not concerned in this book.

‡ See page 73.

§ See page 80.

and moving force of the Peasant League. I have always been close to these peasants from the start. The word peasant, *camponês*, which denotes the most important group of persons directly connected with the land, is a pure word with a straightforward etymology: *campo* – countryside – *camponês*. Nevertheless the word was never spoken save in progressive and Marxist circles, and only written in left-wing journals and reviews. The mass-circulation papers – the so-called 'balanced press' – did not use it; nor was it ever uttered in high circles, conferences on agricultural problems, in the senate houses and democratic assemblies, nor – notably – by the big landowners or their associates. It was like the word Abolition which used to bring the worst insults and imprecations raining down on Joaquim Negro the liberal-monarchist, anti-slavery champion. Whoever uttered the word peasant was proscribed, singled out as a target for the wrath of the ruling classes and the *latifundistas* and their henchmen, scribes and casuists.

Portuguese, like its sister language Spanish, possesses about a dozen more sonorous synonyms for the same word, and inversely it has about another dozen derogatory synonyms too: 'farm-hand', '*rurícola*', 'agricultural worker', '*foreiro*', 'tenant', 'cottager', for example.

When after 1955 I began to use the word in the Pernambuco State Legislative Assembly, I sensed the ill-ease it generated among the other representatives, nearly all of whom were rich landowners. In fact the only woman delegate elected for that year, a public schoolteacher, requested me to use a less aggressive term; and when I asked her what word she considered more appropriate for use in the assembly building, she suggested *rurícola*.* I then replied that I regretted I couldn't take up her suggestion; not only because the peasants had never heard of the word, but also because it was stressed on the antepenultimate syllable and was hard to say.

*The word has about the weight of 'rural citizen'.

'Your suggestion, Madam, indicates that you have never been a rural teacher.'

'Then think of a less aggressive word. I can see the time coming when someone is going to take a shot at you in here...'

'I prefer to take that risk rather than abdicate on a principle. If the word peasant upsets these landed gentlemen so much, that's a good sign. It means the word already has a political content. It's a word that defines a commitment, a political position.'

I later discovered that the word peasant was pregnant with even richer meaning. It wasn't simply a name or descriptive term, but an ideological word. You only had to mention it to call up memories of movements and organized struggles against other landowners in other countries and times; for example the German peasant wars.

In its eagerness to smear the Pernambuco Tenants' Association as a subversive and dangerous thing, the reactionary press featured it under the heading 'Peasant League' on the crime pages. An attempt was thus made to characterize the association as illegal; which failed because the movement had clear, defined and concrete objectives firmly within the existing law. Besides, historical circumstances favoured the emergence of such organizations.

By one of those paradoxes life throws up from time to time, the word I'm discussing – which was supposed to stay firmly on the police page as representing a threat to public decency and order – soon gathered such strength and importance that it moved first to the political pages and finally into the international columns. Before long it was being spoken everywhere and eventually it came to be used by the peasants themselves as a term of respect for a loyal, courageous workmate as opposed to a coward. The former was called a peasant, the second a *latifundiário*. Thus the word *latifundiário* also acquired an ideological basis and came to mean not only the owner of vast estates but also a small farmer or landless peasant who had betrayed his comrades or refused to involve himself with the League. At one point the *latifundio* owners preferred not to be called by their usual name and rejected the term vehemently, ashamed of it and offended by it; just like the bourgeois who for a long time now has preferred the name of businessman, industrialist or progressive.

This phenomenon always used to remind me of the rage I remember seeing in a black woman's eyes who spoke contemptuously of the fact that her forefathers were slaves and who had come to detest her own colour.

The majority of the Brazilian peasantry is made up not of hired labourers but of true peasants or serfs. In saying this I am contradicting the thesis of Caio Prado Junior, the admirable author of *The Formation of Modern Brazil* for whom the term peasant applied to the Brazilian situation is inaccurate because of the absence of detailed studies of land-and-labour relationships in the country since the earliest days of colonization. In his latest work he reaffirms this theory, and I agree absolutely with Caio Prado that it is impossible to speak of a Brazilian feudalism such as existed in medieval Europe or Tsarist Russia at the turn of the last century. This would indeed be incorrect. But to my mind it is equally incorrect to go on from this premise to claim that the overwhelming majority of the rural population of Brazil is not peasant on the grounds that the land-tenure system (e.g. the system of half or third rent in kind which is the prevailing mode of exploitation in the country) represents a kind of formal employer–employee contract with wages paid in kind. Such an interpretation begs many questions.

Words, as semantics shows, change meaning with changes of place and time, as was demonstrated of the word peasant in the previous chapter. Consequently I'm convinced that when experts on the Brazilian agrarian problem use the terms feudalism, or feudal survivals, they are not using the words in their literal, etymological sense but ideologically or politically. It would indeed be unthinkable that these experts, many of whom are in fact extremely learned, would allow comparisons between economic and social situations which are self-evidently quite distinct from one another. With this in mind we can now approach the several types of exploitation and oppression inflicted on the Brazilian peasant which define him as a peasant in the true sense of the word, although naturally I do not intend to tread the whole *via crucis* charted by the 'lords of the land' in their attempts to feudalize and drink to the dregs the last drop of their serfs' and slaves' sweat.

Let us begin with *parceria* or rent in kind.

A *parceiro* is a peasant who rents a plot of land in return for part of his product which he hands over to the landlord. The owner or *latifundiário* is called the 'colonel' in some parts of Brazil, especially in the North-East. *Parceria* is a type of peasant exploitation whose origins go back to remotest times, earlier even than feudalism itself, which it has survived. It goes hand in hand with slavery. Capitalism assimilates it readily.

In Brazil it appears under every kind of shape and form according to the region; and within any given region it varies according to the type of farming and the severity and power of the landowners. The predominant form is *meação* or half-sharing, after which come *terça* (third shares) and *quarta* (quarter shares) the lowest type of rent in kind. As a rule the owner settles on a certain type of farming to assure himself a return from the rent, and this type of farming depends in turn on the potential of the soil in the area. In the intermediate zones and *agreste* the crops are usually maize, beans and cotton; around São Francisco rice and onions predominate, and so on.

But with the rapid rise in the value of land in recent years — due to the opening of roads and improved transport and commercial possibilities, as well as to the increase in population and other factors not connected with the region itself – the cleverest and most grasping landowners have been devising new sorts of exploitation.

Cotton is a typical example. There now prevails in the *agreste* an even more unjust system of renting than the older ones: payment of rent in terms of kilos of cotton per hectare. This is an obvious trick and it always works against the peasant who is a newcomer, tired-out from other exhausted or exhausting soil. It often happens that the amount of cotton picked falls short of the amount agreed for the rent, in which case the peasant must find the difference from elsewhere or be evicted. If he doesn't have money from the sale of a pig or steer and his landlord is 'humane' he can agree to leave the deficit to be paid the following year. On top of this payment of half or third of the produce in rent, the owner also has what is known as *forragem* or grazing rights, 'rights' which allow him to put his cattle out to graze on the maize-straw, beanstalks and green leaves and pods of grass cotton. These pods could have given the peasant a few kilos of cotton to change for some flour or pieces of beef; but the cattle devour everything leaving only the *cambão* or maize stalks and the bare cotton stems, while the peasant must stand by in despair, knowing he is going hungry so his master can fatten his cattle. He does what he can to keep a little plot going on the banks of a water-hole or ditch to feed his horse which would otherwise have no grazing; but if he fails life gets hard because he has to carry everything on his back or hire his neighbour's horse.

This is how he goes on, year in year out. If he goes down the country, say from the North-East to Rio Grande do Sul, the spoils system is always the same, although it may vary slightly: its pace may be different, it may be more refined or elaborate. Whatever its name its essence is permanent: it is a way of exploiting the peasant, of trapping him, subjugating him, squeezing the last drop of sweat and crumb of hope out of him.

Here is an example. Rio Grande do Sul is not simply a land of big ranches, beef and grapes. It was once also wheatland; but the trusts came and put an end to wheat-farming there and stopped the flour mills, so production stagnated and there was no more incentive to work. The granary weevils took over, the wheat disappeared and the darnel-weed took its place.

Rio Grande do Sul is also a rich rice-growing area where rice is grown by the *parceria* system. The owner of low-lying land establishes the following 'contract' with the peasant. He provides the land, the water, seed, manure and the machine needed to prepare the soil. He also gives him a cash advance. At harvest time the landlord receives the whole crop and takes from it so much for the rent, so much for irrigation, a percentage for the machinery, another for threshing the grain, subtracts the cash advanced the previous year to stop his serf starving to death, and what is left is divided into two equal halves. ... Such is the half-share system. The owner thus makes a fantastic profit and the peasant is left with a handful of miserable rice.

In São Paulo State – despite the fact that it is the most advanced state in the country – *parceria* is agreed by written contracts drawn up with all sorts of solemn guarantees. The contract provides for obligatory days of *cambão* or unpaid labour, of which more later. The system is fundamentally a feudal inheritance maintained without any kind of scruple by the São Paulo coffee-growers who represent the most powerful and wealthy landowning bourgeoisie in the country.

The *parceria* system appears under many different forms in Brazil but all one needs to bear in mind is the certainty that none of these variants ever works to the peasant's advantage. But *parceria* exists not only in connection with crop-growing; it also affects livestock, meat produce such as beef, pork, goats and poultry. In the wooded zone, intermediate and *agreste* the rent is usually half of the total produce: full-grown chickens are turned in for pullets or chicks on a fifty-fifty basis. The eggs are also divided into equal shares. Cattle, pigs and goats give a better yield for persons paying half-share rent: a bullock is exchanged for a calf. Its value is calculated (always by the owner) at the moment the peasant receives it, and again when he returns it to the owner; then the first value is taken from the second and the difference halved. The peasant takes his share in money. He never sees the money because he's always in debt to the owner anyway. He also has the job of rearing the livestock on his own land, and has to make sure the animal isn't stolen and doesn't fall sick; so the risk is entirely his. The same conditions apply with goats and pigs.

In the *sertão* the contract between ranch-owner and cowhand is different – or was different, since times change. The cowhand used to look after his master's cattle for five years, a job which took up the whole of his time, especially in a region where life is difficult and rainfall, grazing and watering are uncertain. In return he used to receive one quarter of the calves and then would set up on his own. Such was the system in the good old days when there was land for all; but such luxuries are now impossible. The *latifundio* has been transformed and business is now conducted differently. The estates were sometimes split up among the family heirs, and ownership rights were gradually defined – some gaining more land, others less – via a series of bitter conflicts solved by ambushes and gunshots or daggers in the middle of fiestas in the dusty one-street towns of the *sertão*, clustered about their inevitable tall church. Then came the fences which destroyed the hopes of the peasants of the North-East. These fences of barbed wire or wattle or sometimes of stone came to put limits to the unlimited. The effect was more or less the same as enclosure, save that land-enclosure almost always represents replacement of agriculture by sheep-farming to provide wool for industry, whereas fencing on the *sertão* is designed to prevent the inhabitants' access to common grazing for their goats, their basic source of food.

Just as enclosure ended subsistence farming in Europe – especially in England – and forced the peasantry into the new industrial centres, fencing on the *sertão* destroyed the goats – the peasants' livelihood, which can stand drought like the mule – and drove them south to São Paulo in search of a better life.

Let us now turn to the case of the *arrendatário* or tenant. In the North-East he is called *foreiro*, because he pays a *fôro* – a sum of money in return for the use of his land. The *foreiros* lived side by side with the slaves, and their numbers multiplied greatly after Abolition. As the sugar plantations declined the planters let out more and more of their land to peasants in return for an annual rent. Those who managed to keep going with crude sugar production and *cachaça*-brewing let out part of their land and kept the rest to be worked by hired hands. Many preferred to let all their land, keeping no hired hands at all, and moved to the main town or to more distant cities, thus becoming absentee landlords. The example of Galiléia plantation sixty kilometres from Recife is typical: all 140 peasant families there were *foreiros* renting small plots which came to a total area of 500 hectares, and when the first Peasant League was set up there was not a single labourer or hired hand left. A man called Zezé from Galiléia itself, previously a bailiff on the estate, became first president of the League there.

The custom is to pay the *fôro* or rent demanded by the owner on 8 December each year. The *foreiro* is also obliged to give a certain number of days of unpaid labour whenever the landlord needs him – the number of days varying according to the wishes of the landowner. In that region this was never less than eight nor more than fifteen, and these days are called in the North-East *cambão*.

The *foreiro* is not obliged to go and work these days personally unless the owner requires him to out of caprice, malice or desire to get him off his land; and he could in fact send his son or pay a third party to do this detested obligation for him. The landlords maintain that *cambão* is a duty which benefits everyone since it is usually spent cleaning out the irrigation ditches and water springs, mending roads or servicing other amenities. But this kind of work soon became the exception, since the *foreiros* found themselves working alongside the farmhands, tilling the fields, planting, hoeing and harvesting.

It may be claimed that the number of days of obligatory labour required each year was low. The problem was not the number of days but the humiliation and annoyance they caused the peasant who had to work against his own will, for nothing, for a landlord whom he also paid money for the right to occupy his own farm. Among all the conditions imposed on the north-eastern peasants I'm convinced that though *cambão* is the least irksome materially, it is also the one he finds most humiliating and degrading. It was realization of this fact that enabled me to use *cambão* as the spark to inflame the north-eastern peasant's consciousness and convert him into a political animal.

Land is also let out for money in the intermediate zone and in the *agreste*. In the *sertão* the *parceria* system prevails in its cruellest form of *meação* or half-share. Invariably the landlord, when he collects his rent at the end of the year, uses all sorts of pretexts to increase it, such as the cost of living, the size of the tenancy and improved harvests by the *foreiro*. Another device which became commonplace in the twenty or so years before the formation of the Peasant League was for the landlord to take part of the peasant's holding, a third or half, and to let it out to another person. Measures were also taken to control the type of farming allowed: landlords made strict rules against planting fruit trees or perennials which might become permanent assets; for example coffee, orange, jakfruit and even banana-trees. Only annuals were allowed such as maize, beans and cassava, to name the most important.

Nor was that all. They then introduced accurate surveying so that the rent of a holding could be fixed against its exact area in hectares and the rent for each plot raised in consequence. Moreover they then forbade the rearing of pack animals like oxen and horses on the holdings, unless the tenant paid a tax according to the type of animal. Eventually even milk, goats and pigs were taxed, so the *foreiro* not only had to pay rent and *cambão* but was also compelled to pay a supplement – decided by the owner – to keep the horse he needed to carry his goods to market and a milk-cow or a few goats for his family – even though he provided the grazing from his own plot.

The term *cambão* came then to refer to any day's unpaid labour given by the peasants to the landowner, whether the peasant was a *foreiro* or not. Originally as we have seen the word *cambão* refers only to the very few days per year which the *foreiro* and occasionally the *parceiro* gives free to the landlord according to an old tradition. The fact that the term became generalized is due to the importance the practice acquired, first in the rural North-East and then throughout Brazil, in the period after the formation of the Peasant League. It became synonymous with the medieval *corvée* and caused a deeper impression on people and attracted more hatred against the *latifundio*. A newspaper man from Pernambuco, who later swung to the right and collaborated with the present military dictatorship, wrote a brilliant article on the subject which drew attention to the system at an opportune moment.

In fact there exists an intermediary group between the peasant and the paid agricultural labourer proper which pays rent by means of one or two days' work a week for the landlord. Here too the rent system has taken a turn for the worse: previously it consisted of one day's unpaid labour per week to a total of sixty-two days a year, regardless of the size of the tenant's plot or the type of farming he practised. Later the system degenerated and holdings were surveyed, so that landlords demanded one day per week per hectare rented. Thus a peasant who rented, say, two hectares of land gave the landlord an opportunity for increasing his own manpower. Not content with this the landlords went further again. Tenants of this kind were now obliged, at the owner's discretion, to work one or two days a week for the owner, and sometimes even a whole week – receiving a cash wage for the other 'non-obligatory' days as decided by the landowners of the region. Tenants were forbidden, under threat of severe penalties, to work for outsiders, and were thus enslaved to their landlord.

Of all kinds of rent this is the cruellest and most oppressive for the peasantry and one which costs him all his freedom. If you calculate the wage-equivalent of the unpaid days worked by these pariahs in terms of the minimum wages for the region, the result is enough to make even an imbecile take to rebellion: if he were paid the peasant would be able to buy his tenancy not one or two times but many times over in barely a year.

There is another kind of peasant who has in recent decades come to the fore: the *posseiro* or settler. This type is uncommon in the North-East, where since colonization the land has been held by cane-planters on the coast or by ranchers and cotton-planters in the *agreste* and *sertão*. *Posseiros* are common however in Maranhão in the extreme North as well as in West Paraná in the far South and also in large areas of Goiás and Mato Grosso in central Brazil.

In Maranhão the system is based on rice-growing, and elsewhere on coffee too, especially in fertile Paraná which was called by Saint Hilaire 'Brazil's earthly paradise'. Driven out by drought and the *latifundio*, north-eastern peasants from the *agreste* and the *sertão* fled to the Amazon where the rubber trees grow and there discovered Dante's Inferno. When the bottom fell out of the rubber boom and the green mirages of the jungle turned out to be as much a lie as those of the desert, the peasants went down beyond the equator and scattered through Maranhão where they burnt off stretches of forest, raised huts and sowed maize, cane, beans and rice. They specialized in rice which was the only crop which gave a return of cash necessary to buy salt, quinine for malaria, and alcohol against the cold. They thus risked their lives among the wild animals, mosquitoes and other hazards of the jungle to take possession of the vacant lands in the region; until one day the 'owners' appeared with rifles and hired gangs to claim their 'rights' which they proved with deeds forged in the civil registries by corrupt pen-pushers. Such actions were approved by accomplices who had been 'elected' as senators and deputies.

In Paraná they gave the name of *grileiro* to these men who came with forged deeds under police- and gang-protection to force the settlers off the land they had cleared and cultivated with their own scythes and hoes. Resistance in this case against these legal and officially-protected thieves was dramatic. For whole years the country's main papers were filled with stories of violent clashes. One of the most corrupt and unprincipled governors of Paraná State himself actively supported the *grileiros* in the course of the bitter war against the settlers.

In Goiás and Mato Grosso there were similar clashes where

peasants were massacred for the crime of occupying and using land which belonged to nobody. In Goiás in the Formoso district José Porfírio won his fame leading the settlers in one ambush attack after another until he demoralized the government police and the *grileiros*' thugs who were trying to evict the settlers and steal their land. As far as I know this was the only real victory the *posseiros* won; and its significance was political rather than economic, since the land they won was lost deep in the heart of Brazil, barely served by one precarious road that was impassable in winter. I have been there and seen the miserable huts José Porfírio built after his cause had been recognized as legitimate.

Finally a word about the *minifundiário*, the peasant owner of a tiny plot of land of one, two, five or ten hectares. The majority live under permanent threat of losing their patch of earth which they cling to like drowning men to a plank. None can work for himself alone and nearly all rent a plot near by, when they are not compelled to work out on a neighbouring *latifundio*. This is their inevitable situation; and they become like the parasite fish round the mouth of a shark, always flitting round a rich landowner who looks after them, lends them money and never fails to get their vote at election time.

The *latifundio* needs the *minifundio* just as an ox needs the ani-bird to pull out ticks; so the *minifundiário* forms part of the exploited peasant mass, and between him and the landowner the same kind of relationship develops as binds rich nations to poor. The rich provide the capital and manufactured articles, and the poor provide the raw materials and return the capital with interest. The money lent by wealthy landowners to the poorer ones also returns increased; and labour is the necessary material the poor provide in return for starvation wages carefully calculated by the employer as if the whole thing were being run on an industrial basis.

One can state that as a rule with few exceptions, wherever there is *latifundio* there is *minifundio*; but the *minifundio* grows by fragmentation. So the *minifundiários* form part of the immense mass of victimized poor, and often live a harder, more insecure existence than the *foreiros* or *posseiros* because their land is exhausted year after year through lack of fertilizers and failure to rotate crops or allow fallow periods. The owner also grows tired for the same reason: insufficient and monotonous diet and excess work. The possibility of one day losing his patch terrifies him more than it does the *foreiro* or *parceiro*, and the private property instinct is so deep-rooted in him that he easily becomes a die-hard reactionary. The big estate-owners exploit this instinct to oppose any kind of agrarian reform; so first attempts to win the *minifundiários* over against the big landowners always fail and the process has to be tactful and slow. In the third part of this book we shall return to the problem.

PART THREE

The Peasant League

CHAPTER 1

The North-East and the League

I shall attempt a brief sketch of the Brazilian North-East as a region which, although forming part of a continent – Brazil – also retains its own special characteristics.

During the period of Dutch rule which covered the whole of the second quarter of the seventeenth century, the North-East was on the verge of being separated completely from the rest of the country. This move was supported by the powerful Father António Vieira, the greatest preacher in the Portuguese language, who hoped thus to resolve the political differences then existing between Portugal, Spain and Holland. Portugal actually agreed to the idea and drew up a treaty, but the guerrilla campaign by native Brazilians against the Dutch, led by the negro Henrique Dias, the Indian Felipe Camarão and the half-caste Vidal de Negreiros, succeeded in preventing the secession of the North-East. This was a patriotic war and one of the longest of its kind fought in South America; and for this reason it is commonly said that the roots of Brazilian nationality lie in the North-East, with their origins and focus in Pernambuco. The first stirrings occurred when the sugar-cane industry, much coveted by the Dutch, began to flourish in the region on a more intense scale than elsewhere in Latin America. From that moment a spirit of rebellion developed there which contributed many a bloody and glorious page to the history of Brazil, and this rebelliousness did much to extend and consolidate frontiers conquered long before international agreements and treaties were made between nations anxious to gain control over such rich and profitable territory.

The intention was to surrender an immense stretch of territory to the absolute control of Holland, which then controlled the all-powerful West India Company and was backed by the biggest merchant fleet and best-trained and equipped army of seventeenth-century Europe. At that time the separatists could justify their cause on the grounds that they were handing over a portion of Brazil in return for peace; that it was an alliance forced on them by circumstances. A school of historians defended the Portuguese Crown and explained away the loss of the North-East arguing that it was a strategic solution for Portugal. Possibly Father Vieira was right and could see what lay in store for his country – the question is debatable but by now a thing of the past. I personally would rather celebrate the memory of those three brave Brazilians with their muzzle-loaders, arrows and knives, who defeated the invaders in unequal and violent combat where inferior numbers and arms were compensated for by courage and cunning in the ambushes and surprise attacks typical of a guerrilla war.

Such was the beginning of the North-East: native blood shed to avoid separation from the rest of the country; armed resistance against Dutch imperialism in favour of the Portuguese rule they had lived under for more than a century. They were later to speak the same language, use the same religion, eat the same food and wear similar dress; and peasants say the 'known master is better than a new one'. But one day this yoke too would give way to new ones – subtler, more cunning, powerful and rapacious kinds of oppression.

The foreigner who has never travelled in north-eastern Brazil, or had the opportunity to read such serious works as deal with the region will no doubt be incredulous to hear that men need not make a sacrifice of their lives to live in the area. The common image of the North-East is at once true and false, like the impression given to Euclides da Cunha by the inhabitants of the *sertão* who, he says, 'are above all strong people ... though on first sight their appearance appears to indicate the contrary'.

My own direct observations lead me to believe that few regions in the world offer such violent contrasts as this, and yet provide such extraordinary overall conditions for man to settle and for society to develop harmoniously. The Brazilian North-East is not merely the *sertão*, nor does the *sertão* imply a desert in the sense that camels might seriously be considered appropriate for crossing the region's arid wastes in place of the more usual mule. In fact during one of its blistering droughts, someone once put forward the idea of uprooting and moving the whole population of the famous north-eastern triangle down to the South ... as though nature were unconquerable and man incapable of transforming her! There is no unpromised land: any land, even where there is not a drop of water or a handful of humus on its surface, harbours a treasure for man.

The Brazilian North-East could offer men everything: succulent fruits of every species; all kinds of cereal; long, tough fibres; and mineral ores needed by industry. And yet men live there – or rather die – starving, poor, sick, distraught; men who cannot possess that land. Enslaved men. Illiterate. Betrayed. Fearful. Landless. Workless. Humiliated. Without hope. Without a country. Because a country only exists where people can form an idea of its economic potential, geographical extension and historical and social evolution; where they can grasp what it signifies for each citizen and for the totality of the people and for other nations.

It is an incontrovertible fact and a scandal of this century that for more than half the inhabitants of Latin America there exists no home land simply because they live like beasts of burden. Brazil is no exception. In a vast expanse of land which covers nearly half South America, more than two thirds of the population lead a life as primitive and rudimentary as the ox or horse whom they resemble more than civilized men. Eat as little as possible, reproduce at maximum speed: this is the motto of the people living in the vast Brazilian countryside dominated by enormous estates, and in its miserable towns and cities, especially those in the North-East packed with *marginais* – so-called because they are the classes which provide unskilled labour and endlessly seek work which they either never find or which is never sufficient for their needs.

This Brazil, or rather this North-East, is the true face of Brazil. The other is false like the sun-bronzed face of a patient dying of leukaemia. It reminds one of Europe two centuries ago; and particularly of the two nations Disraeli spoke of 'between which there is no intercourse or sympathy; who are ignorant of one another's customs, ideas and feelings, as if they inhabited different worlds, had different ways of life and were governed by distinct legal systems.' Two nations: the nation of the few who possess everything; and the nation of the many who have nothing at all.

The Brazilian North-East offers a good example of this internal disparity and conflict where dialogue is virtually impossible because the rich of the area are too rich in relationship to the poor. With the survival of feudal or semi-feudal relations between peasants and plantation-owners a barrier is erected against the landless peasantry, and as long as this situation prevails a system of communicating vessels is established between city and countryside with the urban trader and industrialist at one end and the wealthy landowner at the other, all three united by identical interests and motives.

This coalition is difficult to break, since rural landowners generally became industrialists or businessmen without exchanging their feudal or semi-feudal mentality for a capitalist one. The distance separating a landowner on the one hand and a tenant or hired labourer on the other is scarcely conceivable. It is not simply a question of the quantity of land in the greedy possession of the one while the other scarcely has land enough to dig his grave: the distance also exists in terms of the mass of privileges which tradition and law confer on the wealthy landowners in contrast with their serfs, tenants, *parceiros*, peons or whatever name is used to disguise their true status.

The explanation of this situation is not difficult to find. It lies in the fact that 80 per cent of the country's arable or grazing land is in the possession of barely 2 per cent of the inhabitants of Brazil. I'm here referring to the best land with transport communication to the big industrial centres. What is worse still is that barely 10 per cent of the area of arable land is in fact cultivated; so that if all the coffee, cane, cacao, maize, cotton, rice, wheat and other plantations scattered throughout the country were put together in one place they would not fill a single state of the Federation of Brazil of the size of Piaui. Between Sergipe and Ceara, the North-East contains a wet belt 46,000 square kilometres in area, of which only 4,000 square kilometres are devoted to cane and crops. The rest is non-productive *latifundio* or under-cultivated land which retains its value through property speculation or as security against the fat loans the Bank of Brazil and other credit institutions dole out to the landowners; and this happens in a region where the population density is sometimes higher than in many a European country.

This tremendous concentration of land in the hands of a few families has grown up over the years despite inheritance laws, because of the cupidity of the factory-owners.

92 *The Peasant League*

With few exceptions the latter have not developed beyond the primitive methods of single-crop farming and exhaust the soil, render it infertile by raising the same crop year in year out, and then burn the land and scorch the goodness out of it. Then when erosion and lack of water set in they abandon it and move on, retaining their sacrosanct property rights. Meanwhile the peasant population goes on increasing uncontrollably and the poor settle on or near these vast estates where they are systematically exploited as a labour supply and worn down by hunger and endemic disease till their life-expectancy drops disastrously.

It is difficult to describe the frightful effects of this tragic symbiosis between the poor and a dying soil. The figures are unbelievable but true. For years they have been accumulating within the impenetrable confines of the *latifundio*, which has been in turn abetted by a corrupt complex of archaic institutions. One courageous north-eastern writer, Franklin de Oliveira, collected these figures over a period of time and published them in a work which stirred the conscience of the whole nation. Here are his most startling revelations: 23 million Brazilians suffer from hookworms; 18.5 million have goitre; 8 million suffer from malaria; blood-flukes afflict 4 million; 1 million have trachoma; another million, *mal de chagas*; buboes, 600,000; leprosy, 64,000; mental illnesses, 43,000. No less than 100,000 persons per year die of tuberculosis. A child dies every forty-two seconds. Every ten years six million Brazilians under sixteen years of age are taken to the cemetery. Out of every thousand babies 350 die before their first year. The average life-expectancy of the North-East is twenty-seven years. More than thirty million Brazilians never put on shoes, and hundreds of thousands live like animals, half naked, in squalid huts. More than ninety per cent of prostitutes are illiterate girls from rural areas.

In such surroundings of death, disease and prostitution we

discover the peasant, the victim *par excellence* – especially in the North-East where the total population is more than twenty-five million, two thirds of whom live in the countryside. González Prada's remark about his homeland, Peru, is exactly applicable to the North-East: 'Peru is a diseased organism. Wherever you press with your finger, the pus squirts.'

No thinking man, writer, economist, sociologist or journalist, Brazilian or foreign, who has travelled in or studied the North-East can do else but utter a cry of fear and revulsion at the spectacle of this vast concentration camp where nearly thirty million humans languish in hunger. Agreed, they differ over the sort of remedies needed. The cautious, the timid and supporters of the status quo propose superficial reforms and appeal to Christian feeling and a vague liberal humanism. Others, more coherent and realistic, brave the anger of the authorities and the indifference of political neutrals, and argue for the total liquidation of the *latifundio* and all its medieval trappings – this liquidation to be effected by an agrarian revolution. As usual there are intermediate positions between these two which attempt to combine reform and revolution or confuse the two. But before the peasant movement developed these were technical, erudite questions for experts, requiring careful study, and didn't impinge at all on the consciousness of the election-riggers, president-makers and other distributors of office. Now it has at last become a subject for violent polemics and debates at all levels of society – stirred by the Peasant League.

The North-East thus attracted the attention of the rest of the country and then of the entire world, inspiring all with enthusiasm and fear. Such was its historical destiny: once coveted by a Europe hungry for the sugar which grew so readily in its rich soil, the North-East has now after 400 years become a source of anxiety, an explosive area, a hot-spot.

The problem is simply that with every generation the land is being concentrated in the hands of an ever-smaller, self-enclosed and self-interested group, and the more it is concentrated the worse it is treated. In this way the black clay, watered by the local rivers' annual floods, has lost its fertility as a result of centuries of continual use.

Thus the marvellous *massapê* of the north-eastern lowlands and the deep rivers, shaded by inga and andira trees and full of tasty lung-fish and turtles, no longer exist. The forests have been destroyed, the land has been eroded, and the rivers have grown shallow and dried up. This desecration of the black clay in order to create cane, molasses and sugar – together with the loss of the rivers – rapidly aggravated the tragic plight of the peasants of the North-East and of the people living near the rivers who were constantly surprised by sudden devastating rain-storms.

Fluke-worms and parasites add to their miseries. Today a man born on those lands is born sick; and if he manages to survive he does so like a vegetable. On the *latifundio* sickness makes the heart grow hard, stone-like, unyielding to the most insistent appeals for better relations towards the serf. The latter's body is wasted with sickness, and since he does not clearly understand his own degrading situation he puts his faith in time and miracles. But time passes quickly and miracles never come to save him from the worst of all deaths: the torment of chronic hunger which afflicts him from birth.

A question will no doubt have arisen in the mind of the reader of this sketch of the North-East: why should the Peasant League have emerged there rather than elsewhere? The answer is simple and logical: the North-East is the area of densest peasant population, especially along the coastal belt devoted to cane-growing. Portugal began to exploit

Brazil starting in the North-East, and Pernambuco was its first rich find. There – like gold – was sugar; but when other peoples came to exploit the same product – notably in the Caribbean – sugar ceased to be Portugal's gold, though the plantations failed to change their way of life. Like the cacao in south Bahia and coffee in Rio, São Paulo and later Paraná, where immense tropical *latifundios* were dedicated exclusively to these crops, sugar became the basis of the north-eastern economy especially in Alagoas, Pernambuco and Paraíba. This state of affairs prevailed from the moment the hereditary *capitanias* were instituted, and this system of concentrating land in a few hands and repeatedly growing a single crop caused a rapid impoverishment of the soil, and slavery and serfdom for the people, with their inevitable accompaniments – ignorance, hunger, disease, poverty and crime. In the North-East this gave rise to rebellions and the formation of resistance groups, of which the most famous – called Quilombo dos Palmares, in Alagoas State – actually numbered at one time some twenty thousand black slaves. Their leader, Zumbi, threw himself off a cliff to avoid capture. All the repressive forces of the region, both the government's and the landowners', united under the command of Domingo Jorge Velho, the famous pioneer from São Paulo, to put down this slaves' republic of the North-East.

These remote slave revolts survive in popular lore, mingled with the guitarists' and ballad singers' brilliant improvisations about the latest deeds of the *cangaceiros* and their enemies, the owners' thugs. The Peasant League is merely an expression of all this violent past; with the advantage, however, of having emerged at an especially propitious historical moment. The League is being reborn from the ashes of a thousand ancient fires, but its fuel is still the same landless peasant, and its enemy still the *latifundio*. The difference between the League and the Quilombo slaves' revolt is the difference between a drop of water, a turbulence, and a whole river in flood. The League is distinct from the old-style banditry because the latter is spontaneous, disorganized and unplanned; whereas the League has a clear programme aimed at politicizing the peasant masses and uniting them in active struggle for radical agrarian reform and ultimately the economic liberation of Brazil.

*

I usually think of the League as something centuries old, but it dates in fact from January 1955 and was founded in Pernambuco on a former sugar plantation, Galiléia, in the district of Vitória de Santo Antão sixty kilometres from Recife – only forty minutes along a good road through the plantations. The *latifundio* is a wasteland in the North-East as it is everywhere else. And on that wasteland a flower was born big and beautiful as the enormous water lily of the Amazon: the League. It developed fast, like flames through dry straw, spread by winds blowing from Cuba. Conditions were right for the League to establish and grow quicker and more effectively than its antecedents like the *Quilombo*, the *balaiada*,* the bandits and the other momentary, confused, visionary and violent movements which came before.

In fact when a group of peasants came to my house in Caxangá, a suburb of Recife, to ask for legal aid for the recently formed Farmers' and Cattle-Breeders' Association of Pernambuco, neither they nor I, nor any of the important left-wing or popular parties and leaders, had a clear idea of what the Peasant League would become in a few years.

At that time I already had a certain reputation as a peasants' lawyer since I'd been involved in peasant cases since 1940. I had also just won my first seat as a provincial deputy for the State of Pernambuco. The Farmers' Association had

* A popular revolt in Maranhão in the 1840s.

modest aims: to set up a members' fund to hire a schoolmistress to teach the children to read and write; to form a vegetable-growers' cooperative for which they needed credit to buy seed, fertilizer, tools and machinery; finally to campaign against the Secretariat and Ministry of Agriculture and to demand the protection guaranteed by the State and Federal Constitution for agricultural cooperatives and the peasantry. There was no talk of agrarian reform, rents, minimum salaries and other issues likely to arouse the *latifundio* and refinery-owners, though such matters were already being discussed in legal projects, presidential memoranda and technical debates conducted at a level about as remote from the ordinary mass of peasants as the stars from the earth.

A minimum rural salary, for example, had been decreed on 1 May 1943 under the dictatorship of Vargas; but not a single landowner in the whole country had complied with it. In fact this minimum salary only began to be paid after 1963 in the sugar-cane areas of Pernambuco when Miguel Arraes de Alencar became state governor with the backing of the popular parties and progressives in the peasant movement.

In passing this is an opportune moment to demolish the belief that the Galiléia Farmers' Association – which was the beginnings of the League – was basically designed to set up a fund to buy coffins to bury children, who die like flies in that area. There is some truth in this rather distorted idea: the project was more the immediate pretext for the Association's foundation than its real objective. The fact is that the death of a child in the North-East is welcomed by the peasants more as a blessing than a tragedy; and burial involves nothing complicated or solemn, because the body may be taken in a little box made by the father or a neighbour to the nearest village or put in a hole at the first cross-roads and covered with a stone to keep the dogs off. It is not unusual to glimpse a smile behind the tears in the eyes of a peasant mother standing over the corpse of her six- or twelve-month-old child; and one commonly hears from such mothers, dulled by generations of hardship, phrases like 'One less to suffer', or 'If God called him He'll know what He's about', 'Would Jesus had remembered me when I was still innocent', and so on. One long-suffering and dutiful peasant mother used to go to the funerals of her children killed off by gastroenteritis, letting off fireworks and rejoicing in her sorrow, gazing up into the sky: 'Heaven's the place for angels. I envy your luck. God pardon me!'

In Recife – a city where poverty and misery are now completely out of control – I know of more than one person who has been travelling on a crowded second-class bus and has offered to carry something for one of the women standing and then lost her in the crowd to find himself with a cardboard box containing the shrivelled body of a child which the mother was taking to the public morgue.

So there is truth in the claim that the Association established a fund to provide a less degrading burial system for its members, since the authorities insist that corpses must be taken to the cemeteries. Every north-eastern city, however poor, has its burial society which is the pride of its members, as if death needed more attention than life. And so it is for them. There is nothing incongruous in the repeated statement by one of the characters in *Grande Sertão: Veredas* by the great Brazilian novelist Guimaraes Rosa: 'Living is an extremely dangerous business . . .' One of the finest of contemporary north-eastern and Brazilian poets, João Cabral de Malo Neto, says in *Vida e Morte Severina*:

> Since death is so abundant here
> The only professions that count
> Make a job or a joy out of death.
> The only land that'll grow
> Is the land that's full of graves,

> And you only have to plant
> For the death that men die here:
> Old age at thirty years,
> Shot down before nineteen
> Or hunger any day ...

However, I didn't mingle with the Galiléia peasants to talk of death, but rather of life; and for that I was with them from New Year 1955 until March 1964 when we were separated for the last time. We talked of unity, of the land, freedom and good crops, of tomorrow and the future. ... There were hundreds: men, women, children, with serious faces lined by suffering, quiet eyes, calloused, hard hands, slow movements, quiet measured talk, monosyllabic, clipped. Fireworks were exploding in the air. Everyone was congratulating me. Rose, daisy, carnation petals showered on my head. Such scenes were to happen time and again; and I would say in reply to this rain of flowers: 'I'll do everything so that these petals will never become stones ...'

I'm convinced, with a quiet conviction, that I did my best. The north-eastern peasants know the word was kept. So do the landowners. It doesn't matter that the journey we began together has been interrupted: our separation is not final, merely accidental and temporary, and we are bound to come together again; because if on the one hand the conviction is strong in us that we are fighting for freedom, on the other I know that tens and hundreds of thousands of peasants have at last woken up to a new life – even though we may have to start again, along an even harder road, to find that life.

Knowing in detail, as I did, the deepest and most pressing ambitions of the peasantry along the coast, I had no difficulty in identifying myself with them. The secret of my success among those masses lay only in living with them permanently and never deceiving them with advance promises which they would know in their hearts could never quickly be fulfilled.

For this reason, right from the start and during succeeding years, I limited my activities to struggling for two basic objectives: *abolition of the cambão and refusal to pay increased rents*. My constant battle was always to break the conformism of the peasant masses which had been produced over many centuries by the prejudices and superstitions which dominated their minds. I started from simple, well-defined objectives of the kind I have just mentioned; and left until later more complex long-term problems like radical agrarian reform, cooperatives and socialization of the land. I was obliged to adopt the peasant's own proverb: 'Walk slow in processions or the saint will fall.' A mystical, specifically Catholic proverb.

Why did I begin with the *cambão* and rent increases?

Primarily because the League, both in Galiléia and elsewhere in the North-East where Leagues were founded after the example of the first, was composed almost exclusively of tenants rather than hired labourers. Secondly we had to take into account the peasant's almost reverential respect for the law, even though the law works against him and is imposed oppressively from above by city-dwellers. So much time passing and so little change – except for the worse – have resigned them to the world as it was handed on by their forefathers, a world where the poor abound, those who can make a living are few, and the rich still fewer. Hence their conformism and fatalism. 'Poverty may be a punishment but wealth might be His trap for men.' 'The path to heaven is thorny, narrow and hard. The path to hell is a wide road.' 'Easier for a camel....' And so on.

A relation of mine, a rich landowner, discovered that some of his tenants had joined the Peasant League, so he called them together (more than a hundred with their wives and children) and organized a procession led by his special saint, and walked in front telling his beads and reciting the Our

Father and Ave Maria. They arrived at the courtyard of the *casa grande* and he ordered them all to kneel down. He then delivered a long speech which went roughly as follows: 'The land you're living on was left to me by my father. What did *you* inherit? Nothing. Therefore it's not my fault if I'm rich, and it's not yours if you're poor. It was all God's will. He knows what He is up to. If He gave me land and gave none to you, anyone who rebels against that is rebelling against God. That rebellion is a mortal sin. Let all accept God's will lest He be angry against you and you lose your immortal souls. You must accept poverty on earth to win eternal life in heaven. The poor man already lives in God's grace. The rich man does not. Therefore you are more fortunate than I for you are nearer to heaven. Why are you going astray, refusing to pay *cambão* and the new rents? Isn't this what we have agreed? Did I invent these conditions or have they been there since Adam and Eve were driven out of Paradise? Listen to me and take my advice: if any of you have joined the Peasant League, leave it now. The same devil that tempted Christ tempts all Christians. The League is in pact with the devil because it covets land which does not belong to it. It's trying to make the poor stray from the path to salvation ...'

Two weeks later, since none of the tenants already in the League was moved by his sermon, my relative got the police chief to put them in the local jail. I had to take out a habeas corpus writ to free them. ... It was an obvious sign that hunger for liberty is stronger than a sermon; that the League was on the move.

I spoke earlier of the peasant's respect for law. This respect is so deep-rooted in him that one has to provide concrete evidence that he gets no advantage at all from accepting it. So the first thing we had to do was to take the least conformist of the peasants and show them the text of the law which says that anyone demanding *cambão* or unpaid labour from another person is liable to a fine or imprisonment. Only then could we induce them to rebel and resist, although their rebellion took time to develop and did not progress smoothly or uniformly. It started first on the estates of the powerful *latifundio*-owners where the landowners were almost always absent, and later extended to lands belonging to other rich and well-organized landowners. Some owners acted quickly and abolished *cambão* before the League reached their property. Many managed to impose rent increases to offset their loss; and other cleverer landowners put pressures on their tenants to reduce them to hired labourers. The latter move intensified the struggle because the conditions of a hired labourer are a good deal worse than those of a tenant, since the labourer is deprived of his freedom to work on his own plot.

It was no use simply going up to a peasant and telling him that *cambão* was a crime by the landowners against the tenant and that he should therefore refuse to fulfil it. Every time we raised this matter with the peasants and incited them to resist they asked two questions: first, if *cambão* is a crime why don't the authorities punish the landowners? Secondly, how can we break the agreement we made with the owner when we first rented the land?

I recognized the fact that no landowner had ever been imprisoned for demanding *cambão* from his tenants; but on the other hand no judge could ever force a *foreiro* to work for nothing. The whole business was complicated, however, by the existence of the military, hired thugs, police chiefs, public prosecutors and priests all determined to maintain the old traditions as necessary for the continued stability of local society. This stability has always worked against the peasant masses. Every measure was taken to maintain law and order in the countryside; measures such as forced eviction, and even imprisonment against the boldest and most recalcitrant peasants – when the priests' sermons and official warnings from the police and military were no longer having any effect.

The first peasants to join the rebellion helped to spread the idea of joining the League amongst the remaining masses of peasants, but their courage cost them much. Some were evicted from good plots they had been building up for years, without receiving any compensation for the improvements they had introduced; others were attacked by hired gangs and killed or forced to kill and so ended up in jail if they failed to avoid capture by the police.

For the first time peasants were dying for a cause. Not in feuds against their neighbours over a few square metres of earth that didn't even belong to them, nor in gambling quarrels, nor for *cachaça* or women; but in fighting for an idea, a principle, a political conviction involving a struggle against oppression and injustice. It must have been memories of those revered pioneer rebels which fired the movement and spread it from the countryside to the cities. The peasant masses were emerging from their long silence, coming out of the dreary wastelands to discover a new political orientation. They were abandoning the status of human cattle, of picturesque rustics, and breaking the centuries-long spell of slavery. The whole process went on by fits and starts, with acts of heroism and collapses and betrayals alternating. But since life is stronger than death, hope was being born where before there had been nothing.

CHAPTER 2

The League and the Law

Peoples who have managed to liberate themselves politically from the European powers but have remained tied to them economically, invariably adopted constitutions which though advanced for their times took their basic principles from bourgeois liberalism. Although Brazil did not adopt Bolívar's republicanism and embraced monarchism under Bonifácio, it too was no exception to this rule: the country's first constitution – promulgated in 1824 by the first emperor, Pedro I – was as liberal as the other constitutions of South America.

This constitution however did not reflect the realities of a country which was little more than a vast *latifundio* maintained by black slavery and later, after Abolition, by hired labour and landless peasants. All the other constitutions and laws introduced in the wake of succeeding changes of government and régime maintained the basic principles of preceding ones; but here and there some daring innovations were introduced in connection with the social status of property and labour rights.

But who was supposed to apply these laws? The judges, naturally. Between formulating a principle and putting it into practice the distance is enormous and the obstacles numberless. Whenever you try to apply a legal principle against the unprotected – i.e. persons without wealth or privileges – everything runs smoothly. However, if you try to work in the opposite direction and invoke the law in defence of the underprivileged, justice goes suddenly dumb and blind. There are a few exceptions, but on the whole the people who manipulate the laws are frail creatures whose ambitions are directed towards stability and permanence. 'All are equal before the law' runs the civil code and all the constitutions and law books of bourgeois liberalism, and I took this civil code in my hands and pointed out the acts in question and the numbers of the articles, so that the masses should not be in the least doubt. I argued as follows:

'The law says *everyone*. If it says everyone it therefore makes no distinction between the poor and the rich, the peasant and the *latifundiário*. But do people stick by the law? Do the poor receive the same treatment under the law as the rich? Do the authorities appointed to enforce the laws behave exactly the same with the *latifundiário* as they do with the peasants?'

The audience inevitably replied 'No'. The peasant can sense this inequality in his blood. So I continued:

'What sort of law is it then that can say on the one hand that all are equal before the law, yet cannot apply this equality in practice? Obviously the reason is that this law which was written for all only benefits a few. Who are those few? The poor? Since the answer is obviously no, they can only be the rich. And since the peasants are among the poorest people, the law doesn't work *for* them but *against* them. This law is not the peasants' law because it doesn't benefit them, it doesn't help them, it doesn't protect them. What must be done then? We must create a law for the poor since the existing law only benefits the rich. And what is needed to create a law for the poor? To unite the poor, as it's stated in the *Peasants' Charter for Freedom*: "You cannot take up your hoe with a single finger, nor your axe, nor your scythe, nor your plough. You cannot even do it with open hands because then your fingers will be separated. You must clench your fist to bring your fingers together. The League is the clenched fist because it is unity with your brothers. Alone you are a drop of water. United with your brothers you are a torrent. Unity makes strength: it is the people on the march, the hired thugs on the run, the police overcome and justice being born. It is the coming of liberty. With the League in our arms and the unions in our hands."'

I would then take up the civil code and open it to the page bearing the article prescribing fines or imprisonment for persons demanding unpaid labour from others.

'What is *cambão*?'

The crowd would reply, 'Work for nothing. Slavery!'

'Who does *cambão*? The poor, the peasant. And for whom? For the *latifundiário*, the rich. Now I would like to hear of a rich landowner's having been tried, imprisoned or fined on account of *cambão*.'

'It's never happened.'

The civil code maintains that all are equal before the law. But the authorities who are supposed to apply the code ignore that article. They do even worse when they threaten the peasant with eviction for complaining or for not fulfilling verbal contracts with the *latifundiário*.

Basically therefore the law is always applied against the poor, and centuries of such distortion have created a spirit of resignation in the peasantry and a superstitious respect for legality which we had to break. This we did by drawing their attention to the actual text of the civil code, by constantly exposing the inconsistencies of the Brazilian legal system so that the peasant's enthusiasm for justice and legality was destroyed. Thus we managed to persuade certain strong-minded peasants to set an example and refuse to work *cambão* on the grounds that it was slave-labour and prohibited by law.

The owners generally reacted by first of all threatening the peasant with summary eviction by force, and made a complaint to the police chief or public prosecutor. Occasionally the police chief went so far as to imprison the peasant, whereupon immediate intervention by the League's lawyer would usually ensure his release. This development intensified the whole struggle because the owners would not let lands be cultivated while the tenancy was in dispute. On the other hand tenants who got involved in lawsuits won the admiration of others who had been looking on. But in many cases these peasants, when invited to join the League, would only do so if a favourable outcome for the tenants was guaranteed in advance; and we had to accept this unavoidable risk, even though the judge inevitably decided for eviction – this despite the detailed arguments we put forward to the effect that there was no case against the tenant.

Meanwhile, in the course of the lawsuit a number of things might happen. For example, we would summon the landowner to make a statement before the court, and if he refused we could charge him with default, whereupon the case was dismissed and could only be re-opened on payment of the defending lawyer's costs and fees. However, the mere appearance of the landowners in court to answer questions by the tenant's legal representative made a favourable impression for the League. But the landowners' wrath fell upon the heads of the witnesses; and if they came from another estate near by, the owners there – natural allies of their neighbours – would put pressures on them to denounce their comrades or to refuse to stand in court. We met many obstacles of this sort and were obliged from the start to choose loyal and courageous witnesses, which wasn't easy in the first days. Men are afraid to come forward in any battle against tyranny and injustice.

When we found a suitable witness possessing the right qualities we tried a two-pronged legal device to protect him from the landowner's anger – though our attempts usually failed. First we would request the judge to *order* the witness to appear in court or be summoned for contempt; and secondly we would bring home on the witness the full force of the judge's warning that he must tell the truth since perjury was an offence punishable by imprisonment. Even here the landowner would try to force the witness to refuse to testify.

How many could withstand the same victimization as their comrades and appear in court simply to tell the truth? The cases we tried were constantly suspended due to capitulations, withdrawals, disappearances of the plaintiffs to other regions on the grounds that they were looking for work, and for innumerable other reasons. We couldn't even manage sometimes to keep the plaintiff's sense of justice alive between the time he joined the League and the moment he was obliged to testify in court, due to the pressures, threats and promises he encountered in the meantime while he was living under stress. We were battling against human nature, and against the timidity and impulsiveness which are always strong in the peasant's character.

But despite all this – and even when we lost cases – we managed to win the peasants' sympathy and confidence. Our victory was of a different order : we managed to prove to the peasants that the law was always biased against them simply because it was their lot to be hungry, helpless, weak, disunited and ignorant; while the other party had money, strength, cunning and cruelty. We would ask them what was the cause of this bias. Some invisible force? Something beyond good and evil? And we would answer that it was the power of the privileged, that it was a human thing produced by self-interest. Therefore the law serves the interests of the haves against the have-nots, of the powerful against the weak.

When it happened that the testimonies of landowners and

witnesses coincided and went in favour of the tenant and a victory for the latter seemed certain, the landowner could make use of his ultimate and infallible 'legal' expedient, the so-called *prova técnica* or valuing. This can be demanded by either party or by the judge, and consists in nominating an assessor to calculate the value of the improvements made to the tenant's site during his tenure. Each party chooses his own assessor and the judge nominates a referee. Each assessor presents his findings – which normally differ immensely – and the referee, some easily-swayed court clerk, supports the landowner's evaluation. This is the norm.

The judge, however, can reject all three findings and decide for himself, which is his privilege by law. During the whole of my life as a peasants' lawyer I never encountered a case where the judge did this, because judges prefer to base their decisions on the assessors' findings. Assessors' findings are always preferred to the testimonies of witnesses; and the judge invariably decides in favour of his 'expert's' evaluation since it is 'impartial'. What should be impartiality and justice is in reality a farce. The referee, who is underpaid, can easily be bought by a fat tip many times greater than his normal salary, as well as by the prospect of winning the favours of the landowner who is nearly always in cahoots with the local political boss. The judge may well know about these manoeuvres, but will wash his hands of the business like Pontius Pilate unless he is a man of considerable standing and professional honesty. Since such men are the exception rather than the rule, it is always the strongest who win in the end. As a result compensation for improvements are awarded at a third, fifth or tenth of their just value; and as soon as the judge's decision is announced justice is done immediately, by the amount decided simply being presented to the court. Once this is done the judge awards the 'defeated' landowner (who has 'compensated' his tenant) an eviction order which

110 *The Peasant League*

must be observed within the brief space of forty-eight hours.

Since such legal battles can go on for two, three or even more years we tried to use them to incite the peasants to revolt and to consolidate support among them. We also tried to win them over to another kind of battle which would not be simply legal but political and ideological: the struggle for radical agrarian reform and a political system which would ensure their unconditional right to possession of their land and also the abolition of all the kinds of exploitation now imposed upon them. Many peasants enlisted in the course of the struggle, but some were lost to other, opposed movements as well as through the natural weaknesses ever latent in the political consciousness of the rural masses. Mention will be made in later chapters of some cases of heroic resistance both individual and collective.

For the moment let us consider how certain shrewd and unscrupulous lawyers work to find short cuts in lawsuits between their clients – the landowners – and the tenants. It is an old and well-established custom in Brazil that the landowner does not issue receipts for the rent he receives at the end of each year. The tenant dares not ask for one because this would cast doubt on the landowner's good faith. This institution is an old medieval inheritance which pre-dates slavery and is still in force: it constitutes serfdom of the purest kind. Therefore instead of giving the tenant six months' notice to quit his property or be served an eviction order, the lawyer simply states to the court that the tenant owes three or five years' rent: if the tenant up to the time of the court action has been paying an annual rent of x *cruzeiros*, the lawyer claims that the annual rent is five or ten times x. The peasant now has twenty-four hours to produce the total sum claimed or prove beyond doubt that he has no debts. Failure incurs guilt by default and confiscation of goods. Now that all the legal requirements are met, the judge awards an

The League and the Law 111

eviction order, and although appeals against this are possible at a higher level, they do not entitle the tenant to a delay on the order itself.

There were more traps and obstacles. Sometimes the judicial authorities, bribed with fat tips or promised favours, would attest with all the weight of their professional authority that they had issued the defendant with a subpoena and a writ explaining the basis of the complaint against him together with the judge's findings, when they had in fact failed completely to fulfil this essential legal requirement. In other cases they would tell the peasant that he had five or ten days to arrange legal defence for himself when he had in fact only twenty-four hours.

The credulous peasant would then seek me out after the longer period. If however by some miracle he came to me in time he would neither bring his arrears as a deposit against the court case (since he owed none), nor a receipt for the rent he had paid. The only way out was to fight the case within the minimal period allowed to find the deposit, by claiming that the debts had been paid and that the receipts had not been issued, in accordance with an old tradition whose existence would be testified by witnesses. I would also refute the existence of a rent stated at two or three times its real sum. Then came the inevitable request for an assessment of the improvements effected by the tenant. One gained time by denouncing the landowner as a liar and thief who was trying to collect money already paid and who was asking for rents higher than those stated in the original terms. Such bold and exceptional acts stimulated the peasant masses and they formed into two groups: those terrified by the prospect of suffering similar retaliatory action from the landowners, and others stimulated to revolt.

This was how we separated the sheep from the goats. We also showed that the way for one was the way for all, on the grounds that it was better to go down fighting with the albeit distant possibility of victory than to be defeated ignominiously. Despite everything, the League was making progress as a result of this kind of activity. We did not simply stick by the chill letter of the law, the humbug of the legal process and the tactics of juridical warfare but also fought on a political level denouncing social injustice, corrupt institutions and the horrors of the *latifundio* system. Thus we won support from the peasants and poorer sectors of society, even though we lost lawsuits and played a part in getting tenants evicted who had been on their land for scores of years.

Whenever some reactionary judge accused me of being an agitator I always counter-attacked by demonstrating that if there were no *latifundio* or social injustice there would be no response to agitation; and I thus managed to force the judge himself out of his judicial posture into political argument which was my ground. Some wiser and more intelligent judges, who had heard the distant sounds of the nascent peasant movement, admitted that the law did not reflect social reality and should therefore be reformed – a task which was not within their competence. Even though they were embarrassed they had no alternative but to apply the law as it stood. They were at least sincere.

CHAPTER 3

The Beginnings of Resistance

In the second part of this book I made some generalizations about the peasantry, especially the peasantry of the North-East, and argued that they are always the most vulnerable and exploited members of society. I also suggested that once they acquire some political consciousness, however little, they are capable of reacting in surprising directions. What was once immobility, impotence and indifference, is transformed into energy and action.

The examples which follow, chosen at random from dozens I witnessed myself after the League was founded, demonstrate that the devices used against the peasant to keep him subjected to the *latifundio* are useless once he begins to think about his own lot and to realize his role as a human being and political animal. Once the beast of burden becomes conscious of the cruelty of his load, he cannot be stopped. Láo, for example, was a pale, slim peasant, underfed and taciturn, with a large family, and he gave his master two days' free labour per week as rent for his miserable plot of exhausted land. The plot scarcely sufficed to grow the cassava he needed for flour. A certain day had been set aside for a carnival after which he went to his first League meeting, and there he heard debates about tenants' conditions, wages and other rights, and asked whether all these things were written down in the law. When he was given an affirmative reply, he returned home thoughtfully and even more silent than usual.

114 *The Peasant League*

For two days he thought how he might do something to stop his boss robbing him in the future. On Monday he failed to appear for his day's labour. On Tuesday the boss sent for him for an explanation, and he returned the abrupt answer that he would only talk to the *major* about a change in his rents. The *major* was offended and commented, 'Láo seems to have joined the League.' Two days later he sent another message: 'Tell Láo to come and fix the rents.' Láo went and the *major* began quietly 'What was our agreement, Láo?'

'I was to give you two days labour a week for my place...'

'Where are they then?'

'I've stopped doing them.'

'But that's what's in the agreement.'

'It isn't, boss.'

'Why isn't it?'

'Because it's not in the law.'

'The law's the agreement.'

'No, *major*. The law's the law.'

'Where did you hear this?'

'In the League.'

'But the League's not the law.'

'But it shows you the way. It's not the law but it's a light.'

'Well look, Láo, you're going to burn yourself in that light like a butterfly. Do you want a bit of advice from me? It's free.'

'You say, *major*.'

'You're blind.'

'I used to be. Suddenly I've seen everything. Like lightning. I haven't slept for days, thinking.'

'Okay, it's your right to stop doing the two days. But you'll have to leave something else too, your place.'

'I know, *major*. I knew that would come. I was ready for that. But I'm not wanting to live on your land for nothing.

That's why I came. You asked me to come and fix my rents.'

'Well that's what the rent is here: work. I don't accept any other sort.'

'But that's no rent. It's slavery. It's forced labour. *Cambão*.'

'Well if that's what it is, Láo, give up your place then. There's no shortage of people after it. They're queueing.'

'That's the catch in this. Let someone else go through what I'm going through and what others are going through here and in other places. Because they don't know the law. Because they don't know about justice.'

'Okay, Láo, I see you want to finish the agreement then.'

'It's not me, *major*. It's the law. I'm sticking to the law. If the law says I can't do it, I won't. Even if you kill me. I used to be blind...'

'All right then, Láo, get out of my sight and wait for the law. It'll come knocking on your door one of these days.'

'It's already come.'

'The League's law's come, and that's a dog's law. You can wait for the other.'

'The League's law is a dog's law for the rich. Not for the poor. It's God's law. God's remembering the people at last.'

'Okay, get out, Láo, I don't want to see you again.'

'As you like, *major*.'

He went back to his house and every morning he watched his neighbours going off to do their master's work with their hoes on their shoulders and coming back at nightfall. Láo would stop them in their tracks and say, 'Don't let yourself be forced into it, friend. These terms with the *major* aren't legal. It's slavery. And slavery's finished now.' Some didn't answer, and others simply said they'd made a bargain with the *major* and couldn't break it whether it was good or bad. So they would keep going.... Láo repeated his conversation with the boss word for word. A fortnight after the conversation a *capanga* hired by the landowner rode up to his house on a fine horse, with his shiny-barrelled revolver in his hand. He called for him arrogantly, and Láo put his head out at the door and calmly listened to the threats of violence, of his house being ransacked, of his going to jail or being killed. In the end he replied so coolly and firmly that he surprised even the *capanga*:

'The major can have all that done if he wants but there's one thing he can't do, nor can you, nor anybody: you can't make me do *cambão*.' The *capanga* went away, and unpleasant things started happening: rifle and pistol shots in the night into Láo's house and fields, his crops trampled by horses, new cassava torn up, one of his calves killed. ... Láo put up with everything stoically, and he began to see more of the League. Many of his comrades were ashamed to walk past his door, and others would only talk to him in secret. Everyone told him that people were hoping he'd beat the *major* and that if he won people would follow him and join the League. And then Láo would get angry: 'That's cowardice. If I'm on my own I haven't got a chance. If you come with me we'll beat them.'

When the *major* saw that Láo wasn't frightened by threats and that peasants were coming from far and wide to encourage him, he decided to go to law. Before this, however, an incident occurred between Láo and one of the *major's* nephews, a lawyer, which had repercussions. Láo had gone to mass on an estate next to the *major's*. After the service – when the priest, master and tenants were still standing outside the master's house – the lawyer, who had found out about Láo's being there, went up to him, insulted him and suddenly slapped his face with his hand, which bore the ruby and gold ring of a Brazilian lawyer. The people, including the vicar, rushed to stop the attack: 'Enio, you've just been

The Beginnings of Resistance 117

to Holy Mass ...' Enio allowed himself to be led away by the priest with a hard look on his face and his fists clenched.

'I only wanted to teach him a lesson.'

Láo had fallen down, and when he got up, still dazed, with his hand on his cut face, he simply said 'Coward!' Then he walked home with some of his friends. When Enio heard that Láo was bleeding he replied 'D'you mean that swine's still got blood to bleed ...?' He looked at his ring and then smiled: 'After all, what the hell am I wearing this for?'

That sentence became famous, and it travelled.

Láo went to the League and moved to Recife where he presented himself in the Assembly of Deputies with the blood still clotted on his face and his wound uncovered. He made charges; the usual police inquiry followed and nothing happened because the priest begged people 'on Christ's wounds' not to give evidence. Láo stood firm and kept up the fight, and Justice turned him off his plot because, as the judge said, *cambão* is a type of rent-contract established by custom. He's still fighting and is a symbol. Brazil has many like him.

And now the story of old Mata, a story which might without alteration form the subject matter for a major work by Guimarães Rosa or Juan Rulfo.

Old António de Mata was a *foreiro* or tenant on the California plantation, which like so many of the north-eastern plantations had shut down for good. His plot was large, fertile, built up bit by bit with his own hands, and was well stocked with all the fruit trees of the region, a good flour supply, plenty of cassava, tobacco, a little barnyard and a few head of cattle, two horses, pigs, turkeys, guinea-fowls and chickens. Old Mata was a patriarch with numerous children and grandchildren. His house was being extended to accommodate his growing family, while he was putting up another smaller place in one corner of his plot for another married son for whom there was no room in the family home. He was never in arrears with his rents, was respected, a good family man, clean-living, and was going through life year after year in the quiet hope that he would only leave the place for the local cemetery. He had to leave earlier, however – spiritually dead.

Major Edson, the owner of California plantation, presented old Mata with a dilemma: either to have his plot surveyed and rented on a new basis of so much per hectare, or to agree to have it divided into two or more new plots to be let to newcomers. Old Mata fought hard. Everything on that land had been made by him, and he couldn't accept the idea of seeing so much work come to nothing after so many years. He couldn't, moreover, be expected to pay an arbitrary rent for what was now his own property – i.e. the improvements he had brought to the place by his own efforts. The *major* retorted that without the land the plot wouldn't exist, so what is added to the land becomes part of it.

'But it's work that gives the land its value. And the work's done by men.'

Deadlock. Threats. Old Mata then discovered the existence of the League and went to ask its support, whereupon his troubles began.

Mata had two married sons: Manuel who lived at home with his six children, and José in the smaller hut on the edge of the holding, with seven. The oldest was not yet eight. One day the *major* threatened Mata: 'I let the place to you, not to your children. You put up a house for one of them, and that wasn't in the agreement. I want your son off the place and the house pulled down. You've got a week.... If it's not down in a week I'll have it pulled down over your heads.'

'*Major*, that son of mine's a cripple.'

José was in fact a hemiplegic, lame in one leg and paralysed in one arm.

'What's that got to do with me?'

The Beginnings of Resistance 119

Old Mata managed to rent a small and wretched place about three kilometres away, from a small property owner and friend. He put up a 'four-straw' hut overnight, as they're called in the region, and José went to live there with his wife and children. He told his son to come twice a week for food for his family until he could provide for himself.

José came limping with his sack on his back, and returned balancing it on his head. They told him that plenty of walking and carrying loads would put his lame leg right; but his journeys didn't last since he had, inevitably, to cross the *major*'s lands to get to his father's house, and he got a message from the watchman: 'The *major* doesn't want you walking on his land any more...'

'But I'm walking along the track. Everybody goes along it. And I'm only going to my father's place.'

'The track's closed ot you. I'm only telling you, José, like a friend.'

Mata was worried: 'This isn't the *major*'s doing, it's his son Clélio.'

The *major* was by now, in fact, living more in Recife than on the California, and was following a course of treatment for a serious illness which was later to kill him. He had no control over the rage of his son who had taken over the running of the place, just as the watchman's warnings had no effect on the hunger of José and his family. The latter returned once more for food, but never came again. Clélio and two *capangas* on horse-back, with rifles, decided to go hunting and chose José for prey. They missed with their first shot and José got away, limping into some woods which were not thick enough to give him much cover. The three huntsmen formed a triangle with José in the middle. They then began moving straight in towards the centre to find José kneeling with his hands together invoking the Holy Mother, the Virgin of the Conception and the wounds of Christ. They shot him down like a dog, but one of the *capangas*' rifles jammed, as was discovered later, because he admitted shortly before he disappeared that he'd jammed it deliberately so as not to shoot a cripple calling on Christ and Mary.

The news spread and Mata ran with his whole family to the scene of the murder, but failed to find José's body since Clélio had taken it and thrown it on to a neighbour's cane fields – a clumsy move which only exposed his guilt since the neighbour, a relative, denounced Clélio out of fear.

They found the undergrowth flattened, hoofprints, cartridges and José's blood in the middle of the California plantation; but none of this sufficed to make Clélio's relatives hand him over to the authorities. The hatred of Clélio's family and of all the landowners for rebellious peasants will cancel any scruples they might have. Like others, this crime remains unpunished.

José was buried, and Mata, a simple and pious man, cut wood off his own plot to make a rough cross which he planted on the spot where his son had been killed. One day when he had gone with his family and a friend to put some flowers on the cross and say a prayer for José, he was surprised to see the cross had vanished and to find a *capanga* waiting with a message.

'Senhor Clélio says these processions have got to end.'

'This is where my son was killed.'

'But the body's in the graveyard.'

'What about the cross. What've they done with that?'

'There.'

A couple of yards away were the remains of the cross, a pile of splintered wood. Old Mata and his wife picked up the pieces as though they were fragment's of their son's body and said to the *capanga* 'God's seeing all this.' He then turned to go but the *capanga* stopped him.

'Listen to the rest. Don't come back here and don't send

any of your family, nor anyone else, or they'll get hurt. They'll get the same as the cripple.'

'I don't doubt it. But whoever killed José'll pay for it one day. God's hand is great.'

And he went away with the remains of his cross.

After that there were few friends who dared go to Mata's house. As for witnesses to José's murder, none appeared; and if anyone was asked they always replied 'Nothing to do with me. José was as good as dead already.'

Clélio grew confident and tried new steps to get Mata off his land. He even invaded the plot himself with his henchmen to pick the oranges and bananas. He forbade any tenant to visit Mata, and if outsiders came he sent for them with a couple of *capangas* and interrogated, insulted and threatened them. Then an eviction order was served on Mata, and the court case served as a pretext to inflame José's murderers even more. The judge tried every device to keep off this delicate topic of the killing; and any allusion to the subject was ruled out of order.

There then occurred an incident between a neighbouring landowner and a peasant family which had just joined the League. A police squad under a sergeant had appeared on the scene, but Clélio's relatives encouraged them to drive their jeep over to Mata's place – although Mata had not the slightest connection with the incident in question – where they ransacked the bedroom, scattered belongings, broke the crockery with their gun-butts, riddled the doors and walls with bullets, interrogated and beat up the occupants, and killed the young calves and piglets in the field. They then took Manoel, one of Mata's sons, roped him round the waist to the jeep and drove off. His mother, an old woman, quarter Indian, a stoical woman used to suffering, rushed after the son begging them to let him go and trying to hold him back, but failed to catch up, sagging to her knees and clamouring to the

Virgin. Manoel was forced to run faster and faster to stop falling, but finally he slipped and was dragged over the stones and brushwood. His clothes tore, the skin came off, blood poured from his legs, arms and face but he did not utter a sound. The sergeant, corporal and men were highly amused to watch Manoel bouncing along until he lost consciousness. The trip lasted three kilometres; then the sergeant ordered one of the men to cut the rope and the jeep drove back to the city. Mission completed.

Who would go and complain to the police chief when the chief of police was the sergeant himself? Old Mata came with his children and took Manoel back to the house on a litter. When he came to he was lying on a bed of green banana leaves with his wounds dressed with milk from the mangará plant which rapidly stops bleeding. But Manoel was a changed man: his wounds healed but his mind stayed sick.

Another complaint, another inquiry. Mata and his family photographed in the press – on the crime page as usual, which is the peasant's society page. Nothing came of it. Finally old Maria de Mata his wife came to me; a bronzed figure who spoke more with her eyes than her mouth: 'I came to ask you to get us out of there.'

Old Mata interrupted: 'It's not that we're scared. It's just that you don't have any peace. Day and night. People know the League's in the right, but it doesn't help us.'

I agreed, and Mata moved, taking with him what he could, although he carried on with the case against Clélio because he wanted to get to the bottom of it.

Manoel had a seventh son whom he named after himself, and the League built them a house on a new site. But one day, when his family was finally settled, he went to the League's local meeting place, sat down, took out his knife and cut his stomach open. He then pulled out his intestines and cut them into pieces which he threw away from himself until

The Beginnings of Resistance 123

he finally collapsed without a sound. He was rushed to hospital and died in the operating room. Mata is still alive to tell the story. He has many grandchildren and they are growing up ...

CHAPTER 4

Collective Resistance

It was with resistance like Láo's and Mata's that the League grew with an astonishing rapidity – as Nelson Werneck Sodré testifies. Before the formation of the League the peasantry fought back more or less instinctively, but not from political awareness. Such struggles remained anonymous and forgotten because they had little or no possibility of making any impact outside the narrow confines of the *latifundio*, though they still left their mark. The League gave a political significance to peasant resistance so that what were previously individual, isolated cases became examples of collective, organized action charged with greater political significance and bolder in scope.

I shall cite only three examples. The first covers the whole period of the movement's activities; the second its early days; and the third its most recent stages when suppression had given the thing a new strength, like water piling up behind a dam.

Whenever a landowner in the North-East decided to change from one type of agricultural activity to another, e.g. from cane to cattle-raising or from renting to hired labour, he inevitably encountered some easily-crushed resistance on the part of the peasants. The latter would be given verbal notice to quit the land or change their activities, and they were obliged to comply within a stipulated period. After the League had gathered strength, however, things went differently and the sort of conflict described in the preceding chapter broke out.

Peasant resistance on the Galiléia plantation in Vitória de Santo Antão began soon after the first League was founded and lasted eight years, serving as an example which stimulated neighbouring tenants and eventually peasants all over the country. A single example is the foundation of the Acre Peasant League in the extreme North-West of Brazil on the frontiers with Peru and Bolivia. Inspired by Galiléia, this League rapidly grew – in a sparsely populated area – to include three thousand members nearly all of whom were engaged in rubber-gathering, virtually the sole important activity in the region. This League was carefully built up by the Borborema brothers, whose father, a north-easterner from Paraíba, had emigrated to the North-West in search of rubber but had exchanged his machete for a rifle and taken up guerrilla warfare under the gaucho Plácido de Castro who was fighting for Acre.

In itself Galiléia has little significance, being a former sugar plantation composed of undernourished, sloping, rocky soil. There are one hundred and forty families living on its five hundred hectares, most of them extremely poor, living off plots of one or two hectares. Here I began my first propaganda campaign to peasants united in a League. A fair number of them had ballot rights which ensured them some immunity against the local political bosses. The owner was absentee, and only went to Galiléia at the year's end to collect rents; so the menacing presence of the League on his land was reported by neighbouring *latifundio*-owners.

There then began a legal battle after the peasants were given notice to quit *en masse* in six months; but a legal certificate of leasehold existed which gave me a chance of keeping the case open for several years. But I went further and focused attention on the Galiléia case, not only among the peasants who had come long distances to join in meetings, but also among all the poorer classes; and as soon as the dispute became official and local as well as southern journalists started reporting the affair, the cause gained momentum. The landowners' reaction was to turn the Galiléia affair into a police case; but they failed and I managed to turn it into a civil case. The conservative press didn't take long to realize that this was the germ of a movement capable of arousing the nation in favour of agrarian reform without violent social upheaval – i.e. a superficial agrarian reform whence the sacred principle of private property might escape unscathed. If the land were expropriated for cash compensation and then sold to the peasants at its 'real' value (and not its original value or at the value declared for tax purposes ...) then everything would be 'humane', 'legal' and 'Christian'. By this simple device money would find its way into the *latifundiários'* pockets from public funds extorted from the people for exhausted or under-exploited land; and the League, by collaborating in the ruse, would soon enjoy the unanimous applause of the most reactionary classes in the country, the landowners.

We had to oppose a move which would convert the League into a weapon turned neatly against the peasants themselves, though it wasn't easy, especially when one considers the natural desire of the peasant to get freehold of his holding at any price, since possession means liberation. Galiléia showed the region's peasantry the truth that agrarian reform doesn't simply mean expropriation but the devolution of the land to the people who work it without any other condition save that they should simply continue to cultivate it. By much writing and talking on the subject I managed to convince the majority of peasants in principle that they should not be fooled by promises of land to be had at ridiculous prices plus interest on instalments, *plus* conditions preventing them from disposing of the land at liberty, since a series of restrictions and obligations would be included which would incur loss of the land if they were not observed. On top of this they had to work the land! One might as well be a tenant for life as be an owner for a day. Thanks to this question of expropriation we managed to suspend rent payments at Galiléia for four years; and then, when the land became the property of the Land-Settlement Company,* we kept the legal case going another four years until another progressive-minded attorney sympathetic to the popular cause simply handed over the land to its original tenants.

Galiléia thus became famous throughout Brazil as an example of an agrarian reform in embryo; and from its steep, rocky soil and its peasants, united in the first League truly founded by themselves, we struck the spark which spread the movement throughout the North-East. With it we awoke thousands of peasants to political consciousness. Reports and articles published on the Galiléia affair and its impact on the region would fill a thick volume. Fierce debates sprang up during the whole long course of the tenants' struggle for the right to settle on the land they had been renting; and for the reactionaries it was a dangerous precedent harmful to social peace since left-wing extremists might use it to win support among rural workers and so expand this initial movement into something hundreds, thousands of times greater, so turning the North-East into one enormous, uncontrollable Galiléia.

For reformists Galiléia was reminiscent of the sort of feelings prevalent in the second half of the nineteenth century before the abolition of black slavery. As this new wave of feeling gathered strength it would inevitably force the government to proclaim a peaceful agrarian reform 'with flowers'

*A state organization for administering and redistributing land in areas of social tension.

before a popular rising broke out – the same sort of thing as had happened with the 'Golden Law' which abolished slavery. For revolutionaries Galiléia was simply the signal for the beginning of a long, hard struggle by the Brazilian peasantry and its loyal allies, the proletariat, students and left-wing intellectuals, towards a clearly-defined goal: radical agrarian reform, possibly only with the abolition of the *latifundio* and the distribution of land to the peasants.

Thus Galiléia became a source of anxiety for men of wealth and power, but a ray of hope for the peasants. The government needed to adopt a middle position between the reactionaries, reformists and revolutionaries, and tried police violence when they could no longer remain silent. At the same time they tried to woo support with propaganda campaigns like the agricultural resettlement plan, land resale and distribution of seed.

An idea of the importance the Galiléia affair acquired can be had from the fact that Robert Kennedy, then Attorney-General in the U.S. Government, visited the site during his stay in the North-East in 1962. This visit occasioned an incident, exploited by the popular press, which embarrassed the state governor, a factory-owner called Cid Sampaio who had been elected by progressives and leftists. Bob Kennedy was explaining to old Zezé that his visit to Galiléia was suggested by President Kennedy and that the President would have liked to make a present to the peasants as a sign of friendship. 'An electricity generator for example,' he recalled. Tranquil as always, Zezé ran his eye over the group of men accompanying Kennedy – among whom was Governor Cid Sampaio – and surprised Robert Kennedy by replying:

'We wouldn't mind the generator, but what the people really want is for the President to tell Dr Cid to get the police off Galiléia ...'

In fact the governor had broken a solemn electoral pledge

not to allow the police to invade peasant households to settle purely legal matters – a pledge which had won him the votes of the *foreiros*, small landowners and hired labourers in the state. He had then installed a police headquarters right on the Galiléia plantation itself, inside the old master's house which was now being used as a primary school. The tenants had reacted by taking their children away from the school, which isolated the soldiers (also sons of peasants) so completely that they felt demoralized and ashamed. This decision by a 'progressive' governor had been made in retaliation against the tenants' resistance to his demogogic resettlement plan which aimed at dispersing the most militant peasants in order to kill the movement and get rid of the League. The tenants of Galiléia rejected the plan unanimously and intensified their activities to alert the peasantry against this manoeuvre to destroy them. A few peasant leaders let themselves be lured into the trap; but the majority stood so firm that they soon exposed the governor and their deluded leaders.

So Galiléia was soon back on the crime pages as a centre for agitation, disorder, and a threat to the democracy of the North-East's refinery-owners and *latifundiários*. But in 1962 the new governor, Miguel Arraes de Alencar, was elected, thanks to the efforts of the Galiléia tenants who canvassed the whole cane-growing region of the state to raise votes for him as a popular candidate. Once in office Arraes not only carried out to the letter his promise to get the police out of the peasants' homes, but also initiated a drive for an intensive politicization and mobilization of *foreiros* and labourers. The honeymoon period lasted barely a year, smashed by the military coup of April 1964 which forced President Goulart into exile in Uruguay and landed Governor Arraes in prison on the lonely island of Fernando de Noronha.

The struggle by the tenants at Galiléia to keep the land they had occupied for years went off without the extremes of violence encountered by other peasants in the same region.

The Prata Grande is a notable example. Prata Grande is an estate in the municipal district of Amarají, next to Vitória de Santo Antão. In 1956 the sixty tenant families on the plantation were given notice to quit. In this case, however, the absentee landlords (one of whom was an agronomist) were scared stiff by the mere mention of the words agrarian reform and Peasant League. The peasants immediately sought the League's aid and a legal battle began which was to last several years, as in the Galiléia case. An advantage here was that the peasants had good holdings with plenty of fruit trees; and the owners, knowing that the improvements made by the peasants were worth more than the land itself, had tried to sell the whole estate plus two other plantations to a refinery called Our Lady of Carmo. The refinery-owner was a ruthless, calculating man who let the owners know he was prepared to support the tenants in order to get the three plantations at half the quoted price. It was also a move to obtain the peasants' sympathy and stop the League from spreading in the district.

Having acquired the land, the 'Our Lady' refinery had only to evict the peasants before the improvements had been assessed and before the judge – who happened to be honest – could award a fair price in compensation for them. Once the deed of sale had been signed in the notary's presence and the money had been paid – so that the land was now legally his – the refinery-owner sent three gunmen to Prata Grande to threaten the peasants' leader. The latter was a courageous man and met the threat with a group of comrades armed with shotguns and scythes and a fight started in which a peasant and a gunman were killed. The two other gunmen dropped their guns and fled, one with his arm amputated by a scythe.

This was the pretext for a general campaign against the peasants. The refinery-owner immediately arranged with the

Collective Resistance 131

state governor, General Cordeiro de Farias, to send thirty regulars with rifles and machine-guns commanded by a Lieutenant Sabino who was already notorious as a police chief for atrocities and violence against opponents of the status quo. This gang, together with more *capangas* from the 'Our Lady' refinery, invaded the Prata Grande plantation. The peasants without arms or experience of warfare were caught by surprise and those who could escaped into the valleys and forests to avoid their executioners. The others who had no time to flee were caught and tortured. Women were aborted by pummelling with sabre-blades and gun-butts. Neither the old nor the children were spared. Then tractors arrived to pull down the fruit trees and flatten the houses and crops, plough up the earth and destroy all evidence of the improvements made by the tenants.

By night Prata Grande was deserted and only the soldiers remained, making a meal out of the livestock, fruit, beans and meal left by the tenants. They left only when there was not a single fruit tree, house or fence to destroy. Anyone passing by Prata Grande a few weeks later would have been terrified by the miracle wrought by the Our Lady of Carmo refinery: the valleys, terraces and hillocks which had recently been covered with banana and orange trees, jakfruit and coffee, wide fields of *xuxú** and passion-fruits, were now nothing but a uniform green carpet of sprouting sugar cane nourished by the rich earth. The poor peasants kept silent in their misery watching those green canes which had been watered with their blood. But it was all that the owner could do not to dance on them for glee.

Legally the Prata Grande peasants' case was a dead loss, since the indispensable requirement – an evaluation of their improvements – was now impossible. The crime against them was never punished. The press made passing references to the

*A sort of pomegranate.

wretched tenants who scattered throughout the country like dust in the wind. A few years later, in 1962, I was taking part in a mass meeting in the city of Campina Grande, Paraíba, with Elisabete Teixeira – widow of J. Pedro Teixeira – Father Alípio de Freitas, Ofélia Amorim the lawyer and others. A short, sturdy, healthy-complexioned man with a steady gaze came up to me and asked if I remembered him. I recognized him immediately.

'Do I remember! You were on the Prata Grande.'

'Yes, I was the one who cut off the arm of the gunman from Our Lady of Carmo's.'

'And you've travelled so far?'

'You know that Colonel João Pessoa de Queiroz runs Pernambuco. If he catches me he'll have my two arms and legs cut off. I'd end up like a wooden stick.'

'What are you doing up here?'

'When I arrived I was as dumb as a post. I didn't mind working. I thought everything had finished with Prata Grande. I thought the League business was done for the day the police in Pernambuco broke in with the *capangas* from the refinery. But as time went on I started finding the League everywhere. Paraíba is full of it. Campina Grande, Sapé, Santa Rita, Mamanguape, Ingá do Bacamarte, Itabaiana, Pedra do Fôgo ... I'm in the League here, Dr Ofélia's branch.'

'What about the others?'

'A lot of them are living here. Trouble brought people closer together than before ...'

'You had a big setback. It demoralized a lot of people.'

'It demoralized the weak ones with no guts. But the others are strong and keep fighting. I'm in the League because I've got a sense of pride.'

'And because you've got a stomach.'

'Ah! A stomach gives you a sense of pride, but it's a nuisance too ...'

Collective Resistance 133

There are millions like that tough peasant in Brazil and Latin America waiting for the day they will all join hands and start on their long march. We have now seen that the North-East has the right conditions to lead that march. Pernambuco and Paraíba are neighbouring states, joined like twins with the same climate, geography, historical mission and culture; and they are bound to produce a similar type of man with the same habits, dress, ambitions and tenacity. Since the majority of their population are peasants it is among those peasants that we will find the quantity and quality of men suited for the liberation struggles which will sooner or later break out as a consequence of an inexorable process.

I shall close this chapter with an episode which occurred in Paraíba; an episode sufficient in itself to demonstrate that the famous placid temperament that bourgeois and reactionary historians attribute to the Brazilian people is an untruth and an insult to the energy and dignity of our race. Pacifism cannot exist among peoples who are undergoing every kind of injustice to the point where they are dying from hunger.

Inspired by the example of their brothers in Pernambuco, the peasants of Paraíba decided to declare war on *cambão*; and to this end they organized massive demonstrations and marched on the plantations and ranches carrying their tools and banners about the fight for agrarian reform. These peasant marches grew in strength so rapidly that they soon attracted attention in the big cities of the state, especially among progressive groups and advanced students. The landowners thus found themselves daily more isolated; but since they represented the controlling economic force they tried to ward off the avalanche which was threatening to engulf them. As usual a pretext was easily found.

One of the peasants had the idea of hanging a cowbell round the neck of one of the plantation foremen and of making him walk in front of the crowd, and this was enough to cause consternation among the owners' men and *capangas* of the Paraíba lowlands. A cowbell signified the spiritual destruction of the authority of the *capangas* who were working for the ranchers and refinery-owners, and this possibility spread like wildfire among the masses and drew them into the marches against the *cambão* system. Nor was there any lack of necks to hang cowbells round and to parade jangling up and down the streets. In all it was an ingenious move much happier than the one already tried by the Pernambuco peasants in their anti-*latifundio* struggle, where they used to make the foreman or *capanga* get off his horse, drop his gun and shout 'Long live the League and agrarian revolution', whereupon they would march him to the city and denounce him to the authorities for illegal possession of fire-arms.

The *latifundiários* realized that if the cowbell punishment for *capangas* caught on they would be next in line for this 'torture'; so they reacted. The first move was made by the Ribeiro Coutinho family, the most powerful and influential landowners in the region, who owned the biggest cane plantation in the Paraíba river-valley. Fernando Gouvéia, manager of the Santa Helena and São José refineries, received orders from Renato, the universally-acknowledged head of the Ribeiro Coutinho family (although his brother resisted him). He got together a few dozen *capangas* and regular soldiers along with two public force sergeants from Santa Rita district – a stronghold of the League. He armed them with machine-guns, rifles and shotguns, and led them to Mirí where an estate abandoned by its owner was being cultivated by the peasants. He was also carrying a cowbell which he planned to hang round the neck of António Galdino, a member of the League and president of the Peasants' Union. Afterwards he intended to give António a whipping and throw him and the other peasants off the land.

António, however, fought back against this humiliating treatment and was shot down. A savage but unequal fight developed – hoes, scythes and machetes against rifles and machine-guns. A peasant managed to silence one of the soldiers' machine-guns by charging it, machete in hand. Once the soldier was dead the machine-gun fell into the hands of the peasants who could not use it properly. Since they outnumbered the police but lacked arms, they preferred hand-to-hand fighting which gave them the advantage; so the police and *capangas* were eventually forced to leave the scene after an exchange of shots lasting some forty minutes. The manager, Gouvéia, was killed together with two sergeants, a private and a foreman. Five peasants were killed and the total number of injured was fifteen. In their retreat the aggressors left behind their arms and vehicles, and the peasants took the weapons, burned the vehicles and disappeared.

State Governor Pedra Gondim, who was an ally of the Ribeiro Coutinhos, sent out the notorious Colonel Luis de Barros from the capital with no less than two hundred regulars to enforce the refinery-owners' law and order. The Commander-in-Chief of the Fourth Army, General Justino Alves, who was later to become Miguel Arraes's jailer, made a statement to the press about events at Mirí, and put the armed forces under his command on alert ready to intervene. The peasants, however, were not intimidated: no less than five thousand gathered in the small town of Mirí to bury their valiant dead.

CHAPTER 5

The League and the Army

After the bloody encounter at Mirí – for which the reactionaries were responsible as always where the *latifundio* system is predominant – relations between the peasant movement and the army were very delicate.

It had been otherwise in the beginning. I have already explained how the Peasant League emerged in Pernambuco in January 1955. This was at a moment when the reactionary forces led by the Social Democrats and National Democratic Union had once again imposed their own candidate as state governor – General Cordeiro de Farias, ex-lieutenant of the famous Prestes Column, later provisional federal-appointed governor of Rio Grande do Sul State during the dictatorship of Getúlio Vargas, and ultimately Commander-in-chief of the Fourth Army. This smooth-voiced military gentleman, founder and main theorist of the Escola Superior de Guerra, was to become notorious as a clever conspirator and sworn enemy of popular and democratic movements. The League was soon on his black-list; and to destroy it he chose Captain Jesus Jardim de Sá, chief of police of Vitória de Santo Antão, the home of the Galiléia League. This man was one of the most violent and arbitrary in the state police force, and he moved swiftly into action.

One Saturday in 1956 he cut all the telephone wires between Vitória and Recife, stopped all movement of hired cars and taxis, ordered the local magistrate to leave town, and with a corporal and eleven soldiers occupied the League centre where I was present with a few peasants. The peasants were driven out with blows from rifle-butts, and I was challenged into a gunfight which I couldn't avoid. A mêlée developed, I was overpowered, forced into a vehicle and driven to Recife; but a scandal started because as an elected state representative I had certain legal privileges. The chief of police freed me immediately, but the Legislative Assembly considered itself insulted and requested dismissal of the police captain and an official inquiry. The governor was trapped: the inquiry took place under a magistrate – as the Assembly had demanded – and the captain's responsibility was confirmed. But the magistrate, Luis Regueira Carneira de Cunha, a man of unimpeachable integrity, won the hatred of the political bosses and was later barbarously murdered by Aníbal Varejão, mayor of Jaboatão, a landowners' lawyer and fervent supporter of the governor.

The other magistrate from Vitória de Santo Antão, Nelson Pereira de Arruda – who had left town a few hours before my arrest and should have tried and judged Captain Jesus since the case was in his area – was then summoned to the governor's residence and persuaded to have the inquiry shelved. For this he was promoted over the heads of colleagues and transferred to the capital where he is today an appeal judge . . .

The Saturday after my arrest I returned to Vitória to take part in a protest demonstration, accompanied by two of the eight state representatives who had promised to accompany me. Travelling with me were General Viriato de Medeiros and Lieutenant-Colonel Nadir Toledo Cabral, both from the Brazilian Army; my closest relatives, friends and some League members were also with me.

The city was in a state of siege. No less than 250 regular soldiers under a military police officer, Captain Prazeres, and fifty *capangas* led by Alarico Bezerra, the most powerful landowner in the district, had surrounded the League's centre in order to terrorize the peasants and populace who wished to join in the demonstration, which took place in an atmosphere of tension. An incident provoked by Alarico was to be the signal for my travelling-companions and me to be massacred. The massacre did not take place thanks to the presence of mind of one of the representatives, Miguel Arraes de Alencar, and to the energy of the other, Veneziano Vital, who boldly lured the captain of the troops into the League's building and detained him there just when he was due to give orders for his troops to get ready to fire.

At the period in which these events took place the Minister of War was General Henrique Teixeira Lott, a man who was a year later to win great popular prestige when he led his own troops out into the streets of Rio de Janeiro to put down a coup engineered by reactionary groups in the armed forces and the defeated party leaders against the newly-elected President and Vice-President, Kubitschek and Goulart. As a result General Lott became the authentic voice of constitutional legality inside the armed forces against the coup of 1964, which was directed and aided by the U.S. State Department and the powerful C.I.A.

I tried to sound out the legal attitudes of the Minister of War *vis-à-vis* the League, and went to Rio de Janeiro. I well remember our conversation in his office where there was a work-desk with a miniature oil-well on top – a symbol in Brazil of economic nationalism. I knew General Lott and Governor Cordeiro de Farias differed widely on questions of national economic policy, the governor supporting the principle of subordination to the International Monetary Fund. This difference of opinions worsened daily; and despite the fact that Lott was a convinced Catholic and enemy of communism, he was exposed to a systematic press campaign led by Carlos Lacerda, federal representative and manager of the

Tribuna da Imprensa, aimed at bracketing him with the Marxists. So when our conversation started and he observed I was considered a communist in the North-East, I merely replied, 'I'm in excellent company then, Minister.'

A smile flickered across his red face. He wanted to know what the Peasant League was and what I was trying to do with it as a movement. He listened in silence and commented, 'I know what it is not to have land of one's own and to be evicted. When I was a child I saw my mother in the same situation. I'll never forget it. So I understand your aims.'

After a brief pause for coffee he suddenly asked me, 'Is your League registered?'

'Yes. It's perfectly legal. It's in conformity with the Constitution and civil code and Public Registrations Law. The magistrate who handled the formalities is called Rodolfo Aureliano. He is a staunch Catholic and conservative...'

I passed him the official bulletin containing a résumé of the League's statutes and the magistrate's authorization. He looked at it, returned it and said:

'Good. The League has as much right to exist as the Military Club. What do you want from the Minister of War then?'

'Since the Minister has mentioned the Military Club, what I would like is that the army should behave in the same way with the peasants as it did with the black slaves in the days when it refused to be a slave-catcher for the big landowners and slavers. Nothing more. And that the governor of Pernambuco State should know that too.'

'If that's all you want you can put your mind at peace. The army will respect the League, but the state governor has his own police and his own freedom of action.'

After this we said good-bye. The minister kept his word faithfully.

I then started leading peasant marches on Recife with the

double objective of broadening the peasants' awareness of the world they were living in, and of attracting support and solidarity from the capital's workers, students, intellectuals and all the progressive sectors of society.

The first of these marches, numbering about 600 peasants, was organized to commemorate Labour Day. This was in 1957. The peasants fraternized with the urban workers, ate with them and went to a football match and to the theatre with them. They had never before participated in the May Day festivities, and the news spread throughout the surrounding countryside and was reported in the press. Many of the peasants who took part were singled out by the landowners and suffered all kinds of reprisals; but in spite of this the first state conference of Pernambuco peasants was held the following year in Recife with a demonstration march by 3,000 *foreiros* through the main streets and a mass-meeting in the Legislative Assembly building, named after Joaquim Nabuco, the great champion of Abolition. The conference was held on 13 May, anniversary of the abolition of black slavery in Brazil.

Later such marches became commonplace, not only in Recife but also in the inland cities where the League had by then established strong centres. The marches were always in commemoration of some historical date and demonstrated support for some regional, national or international event.

In 1960 the League staged an event hitherto unprecedented in Brazil. The peasants, who were by now sufficiently aroused by political agitation, decided after consultations between their various groups, to adopt Henrique Teixeira Lott as candidate for the president of the republic. Lott was the author of the universally remembered phrase 'The League has as much right to exist as the Military Club.'

Since Pernambuco was the birthplace of the League, and its capital Recife the political and industrial centre of the

North, it was the obvious site for the peasant convention which was held that year. Thus we brought no less than ten thousand peasants to Recife from the interior of Paraíba and Pernambuco, while another ten thousand flocked to the stations and roads struggling for a place – the League was poor and had no funds to shift so many people over distances between 50 and 300 kilometres. The scenes in Recife were striking: the march through the capital's streets was led by General's Lott's representative, Leonel Brizola, governor of Rio Grande do Sul, who was a year later to win just renown when Jánio Quadros resigned in favour of João Goulart. This demonstration by peasants, workers and intellectuals showed the strength of the north-eastern peasant movement and gave warning to the reactionary bourgeoisie that the *latifundio*'s days were numbered.

But the *latifundio* was by no means finished. Our peasant demonstration, with its enormous banners in support of agrarian reform and portraits of important Brazilian and Latin American political figures, enabled the state governor, Cid Sampaio, a fervent supporter of Jánio Quadros, to get together reactionary factory-owners, businessmen and bankers who supplied him with all the money he needed to defeat General Lott, 'the Peasant League's and Communists' candidate' as they dubbed him. Lott was soundly defeated. Some attributed his defeat to his tolerant attitude towards the League, his anti-*latifundio* views, his intransigent opposition to the São Paulo and Paraná coffee-lords, his outspoken sympathy for the rights of settlers, peasants and day-labourers to occupy their land and set up organizations, and his campaign among the illiterate when he knew that between eighty and ninety per cent of the Brazilian rural population could neither read nor write.

After Quadros's triumph swift revenge was visited on the League and the new Minister of the Interior, General Cordeiro de Farias (inevitably), was appointed to apply it. The army began raids on peasant cottages in Paraíba and Pernambuco ostensibly in search of machine-guns, rifles and other prohibited weapons. These raids became commonplace, even though the army found nothing except a few old fowling-pieces, scythes, machetes and hoes. The army also arrested the most active peasant leaders and turned a blind eye on the activities of the police and *capangas* who were now once again active throughout the country. They also made no move against the open traffic in arms between the associations and federations of landowners in the Centre, South and North-East. The protests of the persecuted peasants went unheard in the barracks and governors' palaces.

When Quadros resigned Goulart came to power, and the League had a breathing-space. In the first days of his presidency the first national conference of Brazilian agricultural workers was held in Belo Horizonte, capital of Minas Gerais, and 1,600 delegates attended from twenty federal states. This conference polarized antagonisms hitherto concealed and forced every Brazilian in the big cities to define his position. After this tempers grew daily more heated. A campaign was started to unionize the rural peasantry of Brazil, and was led by such courageous figures as Father Francisco Lage, defender of the slum-dwellers of Belo Horizonte, Father Arquimedes Bruno from Ceará, and the famous federal deputy and public speaker from Rio Grande, Rui Ramos, founder and leader of MASTER.* The gaucho governor Leonel Brizola also participated, and was later to become increasingly involved in campaigns for landless peasants in the same way as he had hitherto been defending the Brazilian economy against the violent inroads of U.S. imperialism.

Because of this polarization, the tension between peasantry and *latifundio* became acute and incidents – frequently

* Landless Peasants' Movement of Rio Grande do Sul.

The League and the Army   143

bloody – became widespread. Father Vidigal, federal deputy and spokesman for the most reactionary elements in the Brazilian clergy, won himself a reputation when – in the national Congress – he altered Christ's most pacific of statements into a war-cry for the Brazilian *latifundio*: 'Arm one another'.*

But they were already armed, and went on arming themselves; and so violence against the peasantry increased.

In April 1962 João Pedro Teixeira, president of the country's biggest League in Sapé, Paraíba, was shot down in an ambush and this crime, like all the others committed against the peasants, was an attempt against the principle of justice. A campaign began throughout Brazil in favour of bringing the murderers to justice. Elisabete, the martyred hero's widow (he had died with a bundle of school books for his ten children in his arms) left Sapé for Rio de Janeiro to plead for justice in the name of all the oppressed peasantry against these cold-blooded attacks which were taking place in broad daylight under the indifferent or approving gaze of the oligarchy. One of Teixeira's sons, less than nine years old, talked of revenging his father's death when he grew up, and was hit in the face by a charge of lead shot which kept him weeks in hospital between life and death. His eldest daughter patiently waited for justice to be done, and when it was not, she committed suicide.

The *latifundio*-owners, not satisfied with such crimes and the fact that they were already armed to the teeth, now requested army intervention against the League, and I sent an open letter to the Minister of War which I include here simply to give an idea of what we were expecting – and had a right to expect – from an army which had always prided itself on its popular origins and the blood shed by the Indians, black slaves and *mestiços* in their war against the Dutch.

*A play on the two words *amai* – 'love' and *armai* – 'arm'.

Rio de Janeiro, 9 April 1962.

His Excellency the Minister of War.

During Your Excellency's recent visit to Paraíba the press gave prominence to the fact that a group of the state's wealthy landowners sought an audience with you and requested army intervention against the Peasant League, receiving the expected reply that the question could not be discussed in such terms. The press added that you went so far as to declare that what was needed was the agrarian reform already being demanded by the whole nation.

Your reply reminds me of Marshal Lott, then Minister of War, who supported the settlers against the *grileiros* and favoured Peasant Leagues on the grounds that if they are legally constituted they have the same status as trade unions, civil servants' associations, industrial confederations or officers' clubs.

Although our constitutions, after that of the First Republic (established by Floriano, the army's hero), state that all citizens are equal before the law, facts show that this ideal is unrealized since there is neither law, nor justice, nor protection of any kind for the peasants of our country. They have always been treated like pariahs, slaves, animals, and mercilessly exploited, sold, evicted from the land which is the centre of their existence, or even murdered with impunity. The civil code declares private property sacrosanct, a sacred monument to the land profiteer. The penal code exists, in practice, only for the poor. There is an infamous conspiracy afoot against the peasantry. The landless or semi-landless peasant represents the majority of our people, and for him the land of Brazil is like a galley or prisoner's shackles round his feet, which he only shakes off with death. It is his home. He provides the soldiers to defend it; yet he lives in grass huts and wears a loincloth like the Indians. His daughters fill the brothels for the diversion of the cities. He goes with his comrades to the church, and the church offers him afterlife as a consolation. He plants crops to feed soldiers and generals, priests and cardinals, clerks and chief ministers, but he dies of hunger himself. Hunger is born with him but does not die with him, because hunger is the only thing he leaves to his children. When he rebels he becomes a

Zumbi or Balaio or Cabano, or António Conselheiro, Felipe dos Santos, António Silvino or Lampião; and then he is written off as a bandit or fanatic threatening the *latifundio* and the 'Christian' family, law, order and everything else corrupt; but he becomes a ray of hope for the poor; a revenger for the crimes which are visited on him from the day of his birth.

Not satisfied with having enslaved forty million of our brothers, the *latifundio* curtails their suffering by setting thugs against them to kill them. It has always been like this. But now, Your Excellency, *capangas* are being organized on all sorts of pretexts designed to maintain and defend the *latifundio*. They say 'Christian' civilization is in danger, that law and order are being destroyed, that 'democracy' is at stake – as if Christianity were what we have here: 5000 per cent profits; life without future for others; old age without a past; gaming; prostitution; the theft of property and conscience. As if 'democracy' were this farcical campaign against the poor, this disguised legal dictatorship, this miserable carnival where the poor lick the 'Christian' family's crumbs.

Organizations like FARSUL,* and FARENG,† and the agrarian fronts have been set up to defend private ownership of the land – i.e. the *latifundio* – so that two per cent of the Brazilian population may control the nation's arable land. Meanwhile only ten per cent of this land is used while the owners take their seats in the Senate, Congress, and state assemblies; or figure on the front pages of newspapers or in television programmes; or give thanksgiving masses or charity fiestas designed to enlist Christ against Marx. The fact is that none of them has Christ in his heart nor Marx in his conscience, because for them the neighbour Christ spoke of is himself, and Marx is an outlaw best dealt with by a Borer or an Ardovino.‡

They invent guerrilla movements and then under the pretext of defending constitutional order (*their* order, and *their* law, and

---

* Federation of Rural Associations of Rio Grande do Sul.
† Federation of Rural Associations of Minas Gerais.
‡ Chiefs of Lacerda's police force.

their 'Christian' civilization) they look for Floriano's army to kill off their enemies, while they intensify their violence against the peasant masses. They invoke not Christ – whose image they display in their houses to deceive the good faith of the humble and meek – but the *capanga*. They organize syndicates disguised with various titles; they set up funds for themselves and acquire arms meant solely for the army – a fact the secret service can no longer ignore without exposing their incompetence; and they murder such peasant leaders who distinguish themselves for their bravery, patriotism and organizational capacity in the struggle.

This is what is happening more and more in Paraíba. In a short space of time several peasant leaders have been wounded and two have been killed, one in Mamanguape and the other in Sapé. José Martins and João Pedro de Teixeira are martyrs in the struggle for agrarian reform. The authors of such murders are well known: they sport machine-guns, carbines and 45mm pistols and move about freely, while the army confiscates the peasants' fowling-pieces which are muzzle-loaded with black powder and birdshot. Soon their scythes and hose will be taken; perhaps they will even tear out their fingernails so they can no longer dig the earth.

If the army refuses to disarm the *latifundio* and outlaw the *capanga* on the grounds that it must defend a feudal private property system, it also abdicates its right to prevent the peasants from arming themselves to defend their life and liberty, which are more sacred rights than the land itself. This is a right to self defence granted even to animals. If the army remains silent in the face of these facts, it becomes an accomplice to them. So does the church. And then the principle of universal equality before the law must be declared a dead letter, and we must return to the old law of retaliation: an eye for an eye and a tooth for a tooth. Or to Vargas's principle: take justice into your own hands.

In view of these facts, Minister, I request you to speak frankly to the nation before the masses despair and rise up to fulfil Thomas Jefferson's prophecy: 'Freedom must be watered from time to time with the blood of tyrants.'

Look to your conscience as a patriot and see that history is not on the side of the *latifundio* but on the side of the peasant. Our country will never be free, sovereign and prosperous while there remains a peasant deprived of justice and freedom.

Consider this letter, Your Excellency, as a protest, not as a threat.

Your humble compatriot,
Francisco Julião

Exactly two years later, on 9 April, another Minister of War, General Costa e Silva, replied to my letter with Constitutional Act Number One, which signified the triumph of the *latifundio*. The peasantry thus lost another battle and learnt yet another lesson, perhaps the last . . .*

*The author is referring to the anti-popular measures of the military rebels of April 1964.

CHAPTER 6

The League and the Church

With the church things happened in reverse. In the beginning the League met with systematic hostility from clerical authorities. Knowing the deep religious sentiments of the peasantry and the constant labours of parish priests to stifle the spirit of rebellion among the working masses, the League always avoided open conflict with the church: it would have been easily suppressed had it confronted an institution then still reactionary and insensitive towards the peasants' conditions since its ties were rather with the *latifundio* as they had earlier been with the slave-owners.

I used to think of the complaint of Joaquim Nabuco, a Catholic and liberal, who in the middle of the Abolition campaign in the last century declared: 'Unfortunately our movement for abolition owes nothing to the state church. On the contrary, the fact that convents and secular clergy possess slaves completely undermines their religious sentiments, and no priest ever prevented a slave auction or the religious practices of the *senzala*.' This does not mean that all the clergy closed their ears to the clamour of the landless peasantry, just as a few priests raised their voices – even in church – against the evil of black slavery. But the system was well organized and was powerful enough to silence a young priest's romantic Christianity without difficulty, or to suppress any member whose conscience was pricked by years of guilty silence.

It's not easy for a man who has spent ten years under the

rigid discipline of a seminary to rebel against the rules when he has sworn to obey them without question; just as it is hard for a professional soldier to break out of the system of barrack-room hierarchies and support a revolt against a dictatorship maintained by force in minority interests. One can thus readily understand why Catholic workmen's circles led by weak-willed priests at first opposed the League: such circles constituted a small and lifeless organization confined to the narrow limits of the parish. The priests feared clashes with the owners who controlled local political life so that the workmen's circle was controlled by a larger, more inflexible organization – the *latifundio*.

When the peasant movement led by the League gained impetus, the cities were invaded by a mass of country people coming not to fairs, masses or burial grounds but to the judges and prefects to demand their rights, or to demonstrate in the streets with banners calling for agrarian reform. As a result the church, concerned by events in the countryside, decided to widen the scope of its activities, and the bishops and priests were split into two clearly divided groups: one reactionary, bent on suppressing the League by denouncing its activities as subversive and dangerous; the other sympathetic to the movement, adopting a courageous, intelligent and progressive attitude towards it. In between these two groups a few priests lit a candle for God and another for the Devil, talking radicalism and revolution to the peasants and secretly collaborating with the *latifundio* and the state's repressive organizations in an attempt to patch up social divisions.

But before things got to this point the League had started out on a difficult path which brought it into inevitable conflict with the *latifundio*. It is only fair to say that the League was able to count from the start on the steadfast support of a few Protestant missionaries from several sects who went about, bible in hand, delivering sermons about the land, seed, ploughs, sowing, harvesting and work, drawing on symbols and passages from the two Testaments to win followers and widen their field of action. It was only natural that a persecuted religion should seek out the persecuted, and the League welcomed the support of such preachers, but always avoided giving preference to any one sect, just as it always refused to discriminate between Catholics, Protestants or any other faith.

The League's only objective was to win the support of all groups to attack the *latifundio*. Without doubt the Protestant preachers netted many a fish, especially in areas where the Catholic Church was directed by intolerant priests in league with the wealthy landowners: such priests were refusing to marry, baptize or confess League members, on the grounds that membership was a sign of communism. João Pedro Teixeira, for example, who was a Protestant pastor, led the Sapé League where the overwhelming majority of members was Catholic. Joaquim Camilo and José Evangelista, both Protestants, led the League at Jaboatão in Pernambuco, one of the most active in the state.

Jaboatão (the only city in Brazil to elect a communist prefect, Dr Rodrigues Calheiros) was the scene of an episode between a Protestant peasant and member of the League and the vice-prefect of the city, a landowner, and the incident is an indication in itself of the level of politicization and acuteness of the peasantry.

Whenever a League centre was opened in a city or town it was our custom to invite the local authorities to be present at the ceremony; this was a public demonstration of the organization's legality. Some authorities would attend; others found a thousand excuses to keep away; many refused on the grounds that the League was subversive because it aimed at changing existing law and at agitating the peasantry against

The League and the Church

the landowners. When the vice-prefect of Jaboatão was invited to the inauguration of the Jaboatão League he refused on the grounds that the League was communist. Whereupon the peasant retorted: 'The League's inside the law. It's been registered. It has proper statutes. You can see them.'

The landowner, however, counter-attacked: 'The devil knows what clothes to wear. He puts on pilgrim's clothes to fool you, but the people look at his feet and can see they're goat's feet. Communism is like the Devil.'

'Excuse my ignorance, boss, but I've noticed that whenever something turns up that'll benefit the poor they tell you it's communism. That way they're stoking communism up. It'll end by winning...'

'Do you know what communism is?'

'No. My law is of another kind, Jesus Christ's, our Lord's.'

'Then I'll tell you. Communism is taking other people's goods, outraging other people's wives and daughters and attacking our religion. That is the law of communism.'

The Protestant thought for a while and gave the following reply which is still remembered in the North-East.

'Well, if that's the law of communism, we're already in it. Look: the poor man rents some land, builds a house, puts up a fence, plants some trees and makes some other improvements. One day the boss goes against him, chucks him out and doesn't give him a penny. So he's taking other people's goods. If the poor man has a pretty daughter, there'll soon be some foreman or plantation-owner or rich man to dishonour her. It's no good his complaining: rich men don't marry poor women. As for the rest, I'm a Protestant myself, and the landowner where I live is a Catholic woman. I can't worship in my own house or sing my hymns because she doesn't like them. She's attacking my religion.... There we are, boss. The League came to finish with this law which you call communism and make another, a fair law, to protect the poor.'

Possibly the fact that Protestants joined the League and made inroads among tenants in areas where the priests were most intolerant, put the church on the alert and helped persuade the bishops to look on the agrarian problem in a new light. The fact is that the church could not remain indifferent in the face of a conflict as tense as that which had blown up amongst the now awakening peasants and the enraged and fearful landowners. Faced with this the church could not stay silent, and compromised with the *latifundio* as it had done in the previous century during the struggle for Abolition of black slavery. The world had changed so radically in the last fifty years that a passive attitude would have been irremediably damaging to the church.

Pope Pius XI had already declared that the greatest scandal of the nineteenth century was the church's loss of the working classes. On the basis of this declaration Father Francisco Lage noted that if the church became isolated from popular movements in Latin America and was turned into an ally of the oligarchies and wealthy classes another later Pope would one day say something similar but more serious: 'The greatest scandal of the twentieth century was the church's loss of Latin America.'

In 1960 a north-eastern bishop from Pesqueira, Pernambuco, alarmed by the advances of the peasant movement, travelled to the South to denounce the misery prevalent in the north-eastern countryside, but also complained that I was disturbing the tranquillity of the region. I replied with an open letter written in a respectful tone to which he never replied. Here is the passage about peace:

There is peace in the countryside, Excellency, I know this. I hate this peace with the same hatred I have for slavery, backwardness, hunger, poverty and the *latifundio*. Of what does this

The League and the Church

peace consist? The silence of millions of tiny children who instead of being sheltered in healthy homes with clothes for their bodies and milk for their stomachs, find their way into crude wooden coffins in the local cemeteries, all destroyed by hunger. It is a peace based on the silence of the peasant woman who is old at thirty; based on the tears she sheds at the funeral of her child. It is a peace founded on the silence of the peasant evicted by the *capanga*, by the police and legal authorities from the plot of land where he was born because he protested against *cambão*, rent increases, interest rates and a thousand other cruel kinds of exploitation. I oppose this peace. That is why I have been agitating in the Pernambuco countryside with the noblest of intentions. I write, speak, indoctrinate. Let Your Reverence read my writings and honour me with listening to my teachings in person; and if any word of them goes against the holy scriptures I too shall fall silent.

There were bitter complaints against the church from its own supporters who did not accept the way in which bishops and priests were being intimidated by or were collaborating with men of power. To preach in church is not enough: such places should not simply be used as sounding boxes for sermonizers who go away to their palaces or vicarages with their conscience in peace.

These complaints had so many repercussions that Professor Paul Tillich, one of the greatest Protestant theologians of the United States – in a convention attended by Arabs, Jews, Christians and non-Christians – deplored the fact 'that the spirit of Christian love is found more and more among non-Christians than among those who pretend to be Christians'.

In Brazil it is not only laymen but bishops too who pretend to defend that spirit of Christian love. An example is offered by the persons who wrote *Agrarian Reform: a Question of Conscience*, a book so deeply compromised with the interests of the landowning bourgeoisie that it was anathematized by Gustavo Coração – leader of the most intransigent and orthodox Catholic movement in the country.

It was these reactionary bishops who gathered the landowners of Paraná with their gunmen and foremen in a vain attempt to break up the first two peasant conferences held there in Londrina in 1960, and Maringá in 1962. Both were inspired by the north-eastern Peasant League through the efforts and dedication of, among others, the lawyer Manoel Silva and the peasant leader José Rodrigues.

I must however stress in all fairness that this and other examples of bishops supporting the *latifundio* do not reflect the overall tendencies of the Brazilian episcopate, especially since the election of the courageous and lucid Pope John XXIII. This great Pope put forward the clock of church affairs as far as he could and hoped the church would abandon the silence of the cloister for the rough ways of Saint Paul, thus closing the distance separating it from the poorest members of its flock. This is why in Latin America the encyclical *Pax in Terra* disturbed the Christian conscience more profoundly and embarrassed bishops and priests who supported the status quo more intensely than elsewhere in the world. Of course there were attempts to distort John XXIII's thought in this or that direction; but the essence of his message remains as bright and clear as Moses' burning bush.

What must the church do in future to help build a world free from the anguish of the atomic bomb and the humiliation of social inequality? Every priest or bishop knows since the last Ecumenical Council: simplify the liturgy, shorten sermons and bring all its authority to bear against systems and institutions which divide men by extremes of wealth and poverty. It is no longer a question of conscience alone but of real action in the unflagging defence of the underdog. Its business is to counsel the faithful who forget their obligations, to give refuge to the man who is fleeing persecution and to

The League and the Church 155

resist – by violence if necessary – any person who refuses to put into practice those principles upon which the church is founded and for which Christ died: to give without asking for reward, to make sacrifices without bitterness and to take joy in the company of men.

CHAPTER 7

The League and the Unions

If anyone one day has patience enough to unearth all the press reports about the League from the time it was founded, he will surely conclude that it was something like one of the biblical plagues of Egypt. The uproar caused by the League in the crime pages, and later in the political and international pages, demonstrates the fact that no one shifts a stone of the social edifice nowadays without getting his fingers crushed. The League became the scapegoat of the *latifundistas* of Pernambuco and the North-East. If there was disorder in the countryside, if a cane field was burnt or someone murdered, an attempt was made to blame the League, even when none of its supporters had the remotest connection with the affair.

The first serious charge against the League, made as early as 1955, was that it was responsible for setting fire to cane fields.

To counteract this manoeuvre I petitioned the Pernambuco Assembly to set up an inter-parliamentary committee, including experts from the Secretariat for Public Security, to investigate the causes of these fires and discover the real culprits. The committee never met; so that whenever the charge was repeated I could do nothing but renew my request for an inquiry. The press always started vociferating about these fires, but never found room to take up the idea of a thorough investigation into them. The reason is easy to find. Dry cane stalks are like gunpowder: a cigarette carelessly thrown away, a bit of smouldering shotgun wadding, a spark from a train, all will set them ablaze.

But the typical arsonist of the cane fields is the refinery- or plantation-owner himself. João Fernandes Vieira set fire to his own fields at Meio, Recife, to prevent the precious sugar crop falling into the hands of the Dutch; and that was more than 300 years ago. Today the north-eastern refineries burn off their cane fields to get a quick second or third crop when the fields have not been completely cleared. On the other hand the plantation-owners were hard hit by the refineries – even harder than by Abolition – and went into decline, to be transformed into growers for the big sugar interests. Consequently they are to be seen, Panama hat in hand, in the antechambers of the Delegation for Sugar and Alcohol Products, begging tearfully for a cash grant; or in the refinery offices asking for their cane to be accepted for crushing. For such people every harvest is a signal for lamentations and breast-beating: end-of-year debts, school fees, promissory notes with up to ten per cent per month interest, oblige many to burn off their fields as a last resort to force the tenants to start cutting so they can collect their share early.

On one of the occasions when the League was being billed in the headlines as the phantom fire-raiser, I was told by an opposition member of the Pernambuco Assembly that one night, while he was travelling in the interior, he had stopped his car to gaze at one of these fires where the flames were leaping high into the sky. His attention had been drawn by a man in a wide-brimmed hat on horseback accompanied by others on foot who were studying the blaze intently. So he asked him what was happening.

'I'm in charge of the fire.'

'In charge . . . ?'

'Yes. I'm the refinery's field foreman.'

The whole thing was being arranged by the refinery.

Another state deputy, a pro-government refinery-owner (also grand-nephew of Diogo Velho Cavalcanti de Albuquerque, Minister of Agriculture during the Empire and governor of Pernambuco in 1870) told me one day, when the uproar about the fires was mounting, that he was 'fed up with burning cane to keep the prices up'.

The peasant would be the last person to burn a cane field, and he is insulted by the charge. Underpaid, evicted, menaced by the *capanga* and eating virtually nothing but stale fish and coarse flour, he is only likely to take to crop burning if he is mentally unhinged or a pyromaniac. This was proved by the fact that in ten years of legal activities there was no record of a single League member having been tried or sentenced for such a crime.

Today I'm no longer so sure about this. Times have changed, and the League is now one of the most subversive organizations in Brazil; so subversive in fact that it was the first popular organization to be banned after the 1964 military coup.

Apart from arson, the League was also held responsible for murders in the countryside. On one occasion one of the most savage of the plantation-owners at Vitória de Santo Antão where the League was founded, went in person to one of his workmen's huts to tell him to get back to work, from which he had been absent for two days running. The poor man came out dressed in his rags, shivering with malaria, with his battered machete in his belt – as is usual in those parts. The owner shouted down at him from his horse, 'Why didn't you come to work?'

'Illness, boss. I was very ill.'

'Ill? Impotence, that's all that's wrong with you.'

'That's not true, boss. I'm married and my wife respects me.'

'Are you answering back, you dog?'

The owner then cut him across the face with his whip and, blinded by rage, the peasant charged him with his knife. The owner drew his revolver and fired point-blank, but missed, and the knife entered him through the navel. Wounded and disarmed the owner tried to gallop off, but slipped from his horse and expired on the peasant's ground. The latter fled – to the great despair of his wife and children – and the 'moderate' press started a campaign and 'proved' that the League had encouraged the peasant in his crime. Whereupon I was warned by a public prosecutor from the near-by town that the plantation-owner's kinsmen had called a family gathering and decided to kill me, as head of the League, in revenge for the blood of another of its 'victims'.

I took my precautions – a life insurance policy, a political testament and a handwritten list of the names of my probable assassins; but the blow never came, and to this day I don't know why. The particular peasant in question was not even a member of the League, but a day labourer and not a tenant such as formed the majority of the League's members.

Soon after this an even more brutal event took place. A peasant had gone to his master to collect his meagre week's wages, and the master's figures didn't tally with his own. So he courteously and quietly pointed out the error to receive the following reply: 'It seems you're calling me a thief.'

'God save me from that, boss. I had the figures worked out in my head.'

'I've got them written down on paper.'

'Well, excuse me, senhor, but you've written them down wrong. . . . It happens sometimes.'

'I know what I'm doing. That's what I went to school for.'

'Ah, boss, even learned people can make mistakes.'

'Mistakes or not, I only pay according to my figures.'

'Yes, sir. You can even refuse to pay me at all.'

'I don't live on charity.'

'I live on my own hard work. That's not alms.'

The landowner then threw the money he had calculated at the feet of the peasant and raged at him to take his dues.

'What about the rest, boss?'

'Here's the rest!'

The landowner then got up and hit the tenant in the face. He then took out his pistol which he never had time to use because the peasant knifed him in the heart and fled. He was chased by the plantation guards, caught and tied to a tree to await the authorities. The authorities failed to arrive, however, and two of the owner's brothers executed him with their revolvers. The two bodies were taken to town with the tale that owner and tenant had killed one another in a knife and pistol fight.

The true story came out but was rejected by the authorities. A brother of the murdered peasant, a workman from the local town, came secretly to my house one night to beg me for the love of God to say nothing because he had already been threatened with death and had his brother's numerous children to care for. So I said nothing, and my conscience is still burdened by the fact that I was forced to keep silent when the peasant told me in despair that he couldn't risk being killed. What would the reader have done in my situation?

More and more peasants were seeking out the League in their anxious quest for justice. And for the majority justice meant revenge – and revenge signified various things.

Some were content merely to force the landowners to appear in court. Others were sure that sooner or later a mighty hand would deal a crushing blow to the landowners. But the hard-headed ones recognized that the blood of the innocent is only avenged by the blood of the guilty, and many of these would come to put their wives and children under my care saying that they only had one way out: to kill the boss and disappear. The owners, blinded with rage against the peasants who were influenced by the League, were taking drastic steps such as destroying their houses and crops so that their troublesome tenants had no way of feeding their families.

It needed tact and patience to dissuade peasants who had lost everything overnight from carrying out their homicidal plans. Even finding them another plot to rent or buying them a place was not always enough to calm their thirst for vengeance. The League was fully aware that the best way to achieve its objectives was a pragmatic way with many detours and retreats.

Our policies gave rise to all sorts of speculation. Landowners under heaviest attack frequently wondered why we weren't attacking the refinery-owners. The basic reason was that the League was not a syndicate or trade union, and the refineries didn't have tenants, but hired labourers who were mostly temporary workers who settled for a while and then moved on for other parts. Secondly, the refineries were too powerful to attack head on: they were like well-defended fortresses and needed a long siege before the final assault; unlike the plantation-owners who had only tenants or a majority of tenants over labourers, and lived on rents rather than organized industry capable of defending itself and attacking too. The *latifundio* with an absentee landlord was a sure and exposed target, and it was here that one had to make a start, as any army might do when faced with closed enemy ranks. This was the correct strategy, and the refineries can be attacked in the advanced stage of the struggle when the peasant movement has grown so strong as to involve urban industrial workers, students and intellectuals in the task of organizing the rural areas. Then the fortresses can be attacked and the refineries will succumb.

This was clearly demonstrated in Pernambuco, which was the only state in Brazil where the peasants were organized so quickly that the refinery-owners were taken by surprise. It was a lightning operation. The League had spent years preparing the terrain and politicizing the tenants and through them the labourers and peons; and the popular government of Miguel Arraes had given powerful support to organizing the peasantry. The campaign was furthered by the enthusiastic support from – and rivalry between – the League, the church and the Communist Party. It was a marathon without obstacles, because whichever of the three competitors got to a place first they would find the peasantry in a sort of carnival mood. No one tried to stem the flood. It would have been futile. The rural workers' enthusiasm for organizing themselves was so great that it sometimes caused curious collisions between League, church and communists, because in some municipalities two simultaneous petitions for registration of a peasant union would be lodged at the Labour Ministry's offices.

It was then that a rather clever campaign was mounted to destroy the League, on the grounds that it was superfluous now that a peasant trade union campaign had finally developed throughout the country sponsored by progressive elements in the church and in the Goulart government itself. Our eager opponents argued that the League's function had been to encourage the peasantry to form mass unions; so we were now caught in a dilemma.

On one side we were under fire from the *latifundio* with its age-old hatred of peasants who organize themselves and campaign for radical agrarian reform; and on the other we were being opposed by reformists who defended the idea of destroying the *latifundio* in principle, but were primarily interested in improving wages and conditions and relegated the land-ownership question to a secondary status. The

League was fighting for both things at the same time, but stressed land-ownership over wages and conditions in order to avoid fostering the illusion among the peasants that any person who gets a wage somehow gets possession of the land too.

The people campaigning for wages and conditions no doubt had an initial advantage because they were backed by a powerful government organization and had long experience of this kind of activity with the urban trade unions. The League had reason to fear that a simple fight for wages would weaken the peasants' ambitions to get possession of the land, which is the basic objective.

Goulart, who presided over the closing session of the great national peasants' conference in Belo Horizonte, realized that there was only one way of checking the impetus of the peasantry: to get them into unions and thus have them under government control. He made a definitive step in this direction by creating an organization supervised by politicians anxious to lead a rural workers' movement as long as it kept within the bounds of a programme dictated by them. A perfect example of such a leader is offered by the docile and demagogic superintendent of SUPRA (Superintendency for Agrarian Reform), João Pinheiro Neto.

To alert the tenants and labourers of Brazil and the North-East to the dangers of this move – and they were serious for a rural mass practically without previous experience of the struggle for agrarian reform and suffering from wretched wages and conditions – I published a pamphlet, *Bença Mãe*.* I had first read this to a gathering of ten thousand people – at least half of whom were rural tenants and labourers – in a meeting held in General Dantas Barrêto Square, Recife, on 2 January 1964, fifth anniversary of the triumph of the Cuban Revolution. The following is the complete text.

*Literally: 'Bless us, mother', a common farewell or blessing before some undertaking.

164 The Peasant League

1. We have repeatedly stated that all members of the League should join the unions, and anyone who joins the unions should stay in the League. We have been saying this for a long time and this statement is to be found in the *Peasant's Guide* and in the *Peasant's ABC* as well as in the *Peasant's Charter*.

2. The League gave birth to the unions. That is why the League must watch over the unions like a mother over her son. They must go together, suffer together and triumph together, and a mother who abandons her son goes against nature just as the son who leaves his mother is ungrateful. This is why the League wants to remain close to the unions to show them the true way and advise them when they go wrong. And the unions should constantly keep close to the League and say to it 'Bença, Mãe' and listen to it. Because the League wants the unions to be strong and healthy.

3. To give birth to this child the League suffered much. It was a painful birth in which the League had to go alone, starting from Galiléia to reach all Brazil. It had to change its name. It was persecuted. It saw its loyal soldiers ambushed and shot down, like João Pedro Teixeiro and many others. It went into state assemblies and governors' palaces; it held conferences like the one in Recife in 1958 and in Londrina in 1960. It called on the help of town workers, students, journalists, writers – from everyone who had a sense of decency and love for the humble and poor. It was the moving force behind the national conference of peasants in Belo Horizonte in 1961, attended by more than 1,600 delegates from twenty states from all over Brazil and also by the President of the Republic, the governor of Minas Gerais, the prefect of Belo Horizonte and Minister Gabriel Passos whose death the nation is now mourning.

There the League cried out in the presence of all: 'Agrarian reform – by law or by force!' Someone there asked a peasant from Jaboatão whether agrarian reform should not be carried out by stages, and he answered 'No. With gun wads!'*

4. And when they saw all this the President and Prime Minister and deputies and other bosses of the republic (with a small *r*, because the word will only have a big *r* when the country be-

*A pun on *etapas*, stages, degrees, and *tapas*, shotgun wads.

comes a popular republic belonging to the people and the League and the unions) whispered together and said, 'We must put a stop to this agitation. This peasant conference is a serious warning. It's an invitation to revolution. Either we throw the peasants a bone, or they'll rise up and take the land. And if they take the land they'll take power; and then we'll be in trouble!'

This is what the fathers of the nation said – the owners of the land, and factories and banks. And they talked together even more: 'This won't be stopped with the big stick. There's a lot of them. The tide's flowing and the social question won't be solved by the police any more, or by the *capanga* or local barrack's sergeant with his clubs and guns.'

5. And then the idea of unions stopped being a mere paper idea and became a living thing controlled by the Ministry of Labour under the wings of the church. The Minister of Labour beat his breast and roared 'I'm the father of the peasant union!' And he said to the church 'You're the mother!' But that was wishful thinking. They can be godfather and godmother, but the real father is the people; and this the people know. And as I said, the mother is the League; and if the two had not joined, the unions would never have been born. And had its parents been others, it would have been a miscarriage and deformed.

6. The people have the duty to support the League and defend the rural union. League and union must stay together on the same road towards the same goal.

7. Unions organize, ask for more wages, thirteen-month payments, holidays, housing, social security benefits, schools, hospitals, maternity grants. Sometimes they strike to force the *latifundio*'s hand and put down its pride. Strikes taste of gall to the bosses, but are candy-sweet to the working classes. Strikes are not the invention of the rich, but of the poor, the workers.

The League, which is independent of the Ministry of Labour, will show the way ahead and tell the unions and *latifundios* that wages and extra months are good things but not enough; that they are crumbs, and that the solution to the problem lies in the land. For as long as there is a peasant without land in this country there will be a League. For land is bread, and this can only be had with a *radical* agrarian reform. Not any reform. Not Goulart's or Kubitschek's or Lacerda's. A radical reform which will not come by legal means but by fighting. Radical reform will bring other reforms in its wake, like a locomotive pulling the train behind.

9. Just as the unions struggle for wages, the League struggles for the land: wages are the cup and the land is the water that will fill it; wages are a promise, the land is a miracle; wages are hope and the land is freedom.

10. This is why the peasant must not be deluded by promises of money, but must fight for the land. Whoever fights for land is fighting for power; for power comes from the land, whether in the form of bread or of oil. Bread means the peasantry. Oil means the town worker. And the two united will be the powder and the match, sun and rain, flag and anthem, peace and freedom. Homeland and future.

11. Finally some advice.

(a) Peasant! Wherever there is a League found a union; and wherever there is a union found a League.

(b) Whenever you go to town drop in at your League centre or your union or cooperative to find out the news and hear your leaders, to make your complaints and ask for your rights and do your duties.

(c) Never forget your best friend is your brother in suffering – the brother who has no land and does not know what tomorrow will bring for him or his wife and children.

(d) Don't listen to the voice which says 'you must suffer on earth to reach heaven'. This is a lie, because the man who talks like that has his belly full and an easy life. Don't listen to people who say 'the world is divided between rich and poor and this is God's will'. Another lie. It's not the will of God but of the *latifundio*, the bourgeois, the imperialist, because they want to live off the blood of the poor like leeches.

(f) Never say 'God in heaven and the rich on earth'. This is weakness, backwardness. Always say 'God in heaven and the poor together and united on earth'.

The League and the Unions 167

(g) Whenever your brother is being attacked by the *latifundista* or the *capanga* or the police, go to his aid even if it means risking your life. This is what is called solidarity. This is how unity is forged.

(h) Work with your brother to see how you can take possession of vacant lands, because land exists to be worked. That is how one gets rid of the hunger of the poor. That is good justice.

(i) If the landowner pulls down your house or pulls up your crops, get together with your comrades and pull down his house and burn his crops. This is Moses' law: 'An eye for an eye, a tooth for a tooth'.

(j) If the *latifundista* puts his cattle on your land against your will, get your brother workers together to drive the cattle off and go to the prefecture and take measures to punish the trespasser. If he's not punished and puts his cattle on again, take the fattest animal and slaughter it on your land and have a feast, and go with your comrades to the owner and his family and eat in front of them. It's no use trying to use the law to get compensation or put the owner in jail, because there is no justice for the poor, and no landowner in jail.

(k) Found more Leagues and more cooperatives and unions to put an end to the *fôro*, half- and third-shares, *cambão*, *capanga* and mortgages and other things that tie you to the *latifundio*; because the land should belong to the men who work it.

(l) If a *capanga* kills one of your comrades, whether he's in the League or union or not, you can kill the *capanga* because he is not a human being but an animal.

(m) Don't hope for much from the law, because it's a class law and most judges defend the rich and not the poor and apply laws which aren't your laws.

(n) Keep your machete well sharpened behind the door to defend yourself against aggression from the *capanga* or police who serve the *latifundio*.

(o) Economize, tighten your belt, buy a gun for the day you get even with the men who killed your fathers and grandfathers with hunger, and persecute and humiliate you now in the name even of that Jesus Christ who was crucified by them.

(p) Whenever a man comes to your door and shows his League or union membership card receive him as a brother and listen to what he says to you, even if he comes from another region or state.

(q) Respect the wife and daughters of your comrades as if they were your own.

(r) If you are a union or League delegate or leader you should avoid drinking, gambling and going to brothels; because the enemy never sleeps and is always ready to catch you by surprise, to destroy you with vice and degrade you in your comrades' eyes.

(s) If you are a worshipper of Father Cícero do Juàzeiro or any other saint of the church, go on your pilgrimage and say your prayers; but never forget that your first duty is your obligation to your comrades, because one can live much more easily without religion than without bread.

(t) Never go alone or in bad company.

(u) Never destroy another's property except when the *latifundista* destroys yours – so that he can taste your own suffering.

(v) Defend tooth and nail your cane and coffee fields, your cacao and rice and your other long-term crops as well as the places which process them, because they were built by you and cost many sacrifices; and one day when Brazil is a socialist country they will become yours just as they became the property of the poor in the Soviet Union, China, Cuba and elsewhere.

(x) When they call you agitator don't be ashamed or afraid, because without agitation the poor can never go ahead. Without agitation the blood stagnates in the veins, there is no life.

(y) If they call you a striker, strike your breast and say 'Yes. I'm a striker, because strikes weren't invented by the rich but by the poor, and they are the working classes' weapon against the bosses.'

(z) Finally, if they call you a communist strike your breast even harder and answer like that peasant in Surubim, Pernambuco, who had his bible in his hand: 'You're calling me a Jesus, Moses, an Amos, a Saint Anthony and by the name of everyone holy that ever passed through this world and said: "The land should belong to all, because light and air and water belong to all and men found those things on earth to live from.'"

And now no more advice because there are no more letters, so we stretch out our hand to the League and ask it too: *'Bença, mãe!'*

PART FOUR

Encounter with America

CHAPTER 1

A Wider Vision

Living a long, hard experience with the north-eastern peasants has taught me a lesson no historical, sociological or economic treatise could ever have offered me. Now that I am living far from that tragic scene I find I can look to wider horizons and grasp their significance.

Reality was my guide and teacher. It taught me that nothing solid can be built on what is merely inside us if we cannot first see and understand with feeling what lies outside us in the world. As a guide it led me along paths which all pointed in one final direction: to other men. And this is why today, far from my own region and from the events which have united me to it for ever, I feel closer to the North-East and understand it better than when I was there and was living its tragedy more intensely.

Whenever I mount a step to try to see more of the horizon I always discover a striking similarity between the situation of the Brazilian North-East and the rest of Latin America. Essentially they are the same phenomenon: latitudes change, but the Latin American is everywhere the same Prometheus being devoured by the same vulture – imperialism.

In my childhood the image I had of the continent was different: I thought of it as a vast area of forests and wide rivers, of rich mines, potentially invaluable waterfalls and endless pastures. But this image dispersed like a cloud when I realized that this immensity was inhabited by men without hope. Then Latin America seemed to me like an enormous cross with its head facing towards the Rio Grande and its foot stretching down towards the Antarctic, and its two arms outstretched to the Atlantic and Pacific. Crucified upon it I found men as slaves, serfs and workers, degraded and persecuted – especially wherever they lived outside the towns on the *latifundios*.

While I was still young I was astonished to find that such men constituted a species apart and represented more than half the population of Latin America. I had already, in my home region, heard the sob of despair in the dirges of the labourers in the fields and in the murmur of the cane and the mills under the heat of the sun and the stars. I had grasped these men's fleshless hands covered with callouses as round and yellow as the coins ringing in their masters' pockets; and these hands stirred my conscience and showed me a way towards humanity.

I understood that to fight for such men was to fight for mankind. I realized that the land was created for them and should not be barred and fettered. So I started out to offer them the best things I had: youthful enthusiasm and liberty. And as a result I was obliged, when my hair was already turning white, to leave my home country for exile – without my ever wishing now to abandon my right, or duty, to leave my exile and return.

I realize that it is no use surveying this scene if to do so merely arouses one to criticize and denounce it with words, however violent; if one does nothing in practice. Latin America, like the North-East, is tired of being denounced in words and descriptions of hunger, or in sociological and economic analyses or bishops' sermons. If all these things fail to lead their authors to concrete action there is little difference between them and the men who simply wait for 'imperialism's corpse to be carried past their door'.

In the last forty years of Latin American history, precisely at a time when oppression has been inflicting endless violence on the continent, an ever higher number of men have managed to win the confidence of the masses. But the majority of these men have betrayed this confidence and surrendered to reaction, while the minority have barely managed to survive, with one foot in the people's camp and the other in that of their enemies. This minority gives little ground for hope; and now they are sinking into oblivion in the illusion that they can stand still – although they know that they lack the courage to go along with history.

This is why the masses are now more and more going their own way and looking to their own ranks for guides and leaders in the bloody and unequal battles they must fight for their own freedom.

What is now becoming more and more obvious in Latin America is the fear of the oligarchies and reactionary military castes: fear that they may succumb for ever beneath the impetus of these masses who are now waking up to a new life free from humiliation and anguish.

The theorists of the oligarchies and military defend the status quo intransigently, and argue about eternal values and essential truths. But they can no longer manage to spin the web they need to tie down the peoples of our continent; because these peoples have been inspired with a vision of the future, the same vision that once inspired Tiradentes, Morelos, Bolívar and Martí. It's not difficult to understand why these theorists pontificate with such laughable solemnity about the demographic explosion, birth-control, ideological frontiers, political interdependence and Latin American free trade ...

While they spin their theories in defence of an obsolete order and precarious stability, the groups who hold power are concocting new schemes for the future; and under the invariable pretext of saving democracy from anarchy, revolution, civil war and communism, they have resort to Bonapartist coups – with the most blatant outside support – against any government formed in response to popular pressures for an end to injustice, repression and corruption.

This is what happened to Goulart in Brazil, to Paz Estenssoro in Bolivia, to Arbenz in Guatemala, to Bosch in Dominica and Illía in Argentina.

These are the countries where in recent years reactionary forces have not only overthrown elected popular governments, but have imposed military dictatorships involving partial or total loss of national sovereignty to foreign powers. Where the military coup is not used as a device to 'save' the situation, direct 'elections' (or indirect where their candidate is in danger of defeat) are tried – all under strict surveillance from foreign agents – or occupation troops wherever the national forces are not strong enough to ensure victory for the right candidate standing for the interests of the senior partner: U.S. imperialism.

Mexico is something of an exception in this bitter struggle for political independence and national sovereignty. A vast, potentially rich and heavily-populated country, Mexico has created an advanced political constitution after the longest and most violent revolution our continent has known. This enabled her to redistribute the land and undermine the *latifundio*, as well as permitting her to nationalize her basic sources of wealth – to the distress of foreign monopoly capitalism. Mexico also adopted an independent policy towards independence movements abroad and campaigns for self-determination.

Cuba's position in Latin America is also exceptional. She broke definitively with the traditional pattern of capitalist democracy alternating with corrupt and violent Caribbean-style dictatorships, and brought socialism to America for the first time. This was achieved thanks to three factors: the political genius of Fidel Castro, the existence of the socialist bloc and the unyielding attitude of the State Department.

But both Cuba and Mexico are still living the terrible drama of Latin America, and both are pieces on the same vast chessboard – whether Mexico sticks to the principles of Benito Juárez and has one day to take arms to defend them, or Cuba has to fight again in the Bay of Pigs or Guantanamo for its new way of life. A way of life which sooner or later will triumph everywhere in Latin America.

*

The growing complexity of social and economic problems is provoking tensions between the capitalist, neo-colonialist countries and sharpening class conflicts within them. These tensions increased alarmingly after the Second World War when the victorious countries polarized into two great camps – capitalism centred on the United States, and socialism based on the Soviet Union. This polarization created the Cold War and gave birth to a new world, a sort of mysterious Atlantis, the Third World. This world was composed of Asian, African and South American countries who were trying to shake off the yoke of European imperialism and to establish their independence.

This world is now struggling for political and economic emancipation; but the United States cannot tolerate any political strengthening of the Third World or permit it to slip out of its control. However legitimate the aspirations of the Third World may be, they hinder the United States' economic programme and its increasingly aggressive plans for economic expansion. Just as England before the First World War was queen of the oceans, the United States since the Second World War has sought to be lord of the continents; and this means there will be no general adoption of liberal, flexible, democratic and popular-revolutionary solutions of the sort men dreamed of after the destruction of Nazism. Because such revolutions would imply loss of control by the U.S. over the Third World and over the European countries bound to it economically.

Two events contributed no doubt to push the United States towards the extreme right and to transform its strategy as 'guardian' of the new nations. One was the unexpected launching of the first sputnik which revealed the astonishing scientific potential and technological progress of the Soviet Union. The other was Fidel Castro's victory over the savage dictatorship of Fulgencio Batista. The United States saw immediately that the policy of peaceful coexistence supported by Moscow would eventually imply a weakening of its control over the Third World and its capitalist allies in Europe. So history had to be stopped; just as Rome tried to stop it with her legions ...

Arms sales, dollar diplomacy, dumping, bilateral agreements, technical aid, the I.M.F., the Alliance for Progress and the U.S. Colonial Ministry (as Raul Roa dubbed the O.A.S.) were no longer enough. They had to be combined with the new U.S. policy of military pacts, coups and armed intervention. Vietnam is an example of this defence of the 'free world'.

In such a situation the idea of democracy is becoming ridiculous in Latin America because the classical democratic opposition has no importance where liberties are suppressed and political parties abolished whenever they stray from the hard line laid down by the oligarchies and their foreign agents. Where justice does not exist and terrorism prevents any dialogue, the people have no legal means of expressing their will, and their aspirations and discontents.

In such circumstances the formation of tame opposition movements merely prolongs the agony. The masses know this better than self-deluding theoreticians who preach for the

A Wider Vision

future. The United States is clearly no longer interested in political parties in Latin America, because they might imperil its policies of economic expansion. For the U.S. there is no longer any difference between nationalism, socialism and communism; and this means that as soon as the opposition demands the nationalization of basic sources of wealth, control over the export of profits, an independent foreign policy, agrarian reform and other popular measures, the threatened oligarchies cry out for the safety of the 'free world' and 'Western, Christian civilization'.

In our situation it is impossible to imagine any legal opposition movement opposed to the interests of the big international consortiums – mostly based on the U.S. – because the oligarchies and military are becoming daily more closely linked to these consortiums. The Military Institute in Brazil calls these links 'the policy of interdependence'; and this means inevitably that there is no patriotic resistance to this policy save in the struggle for power.

Which also means there is no longer room for the classical tolerated opposition party with its traditional complicity and indecisiveness. We now need a popular movement based on the unshakable unity of the progressive and revolutionary forces, with a clearly defined objective: the overthrow of U.S. imperialism.

*

In their long, bloody march towards independence the Latin American peoples were inspired by the generous ideas gathered by the first liberators in Europe, or transmitted to them on the same ships as brought the militia captains, soldiers and cannons whose business it was to maintain the empires and continue the plundering.

'The American world's revolution in 1825,' Bernardo Monteagudo states was the result of eighteenth-century ideas; but the soldiers who carried it out were born here in humble circumstances, and were sons of the people, of that *canaille* which achieved glory in the fall of the Bastille. Europe and North America stood aside as impassive witnesses to the struggle, as Bolívar himself recognized. Hence Martí's terse phrase in connection with the independence movement: 'Neither Rousseau, nor Washington gave birth to your America: it came from within.'

In the same way as the first liberators of South America sought abroad for their exotic and dangerous new ideas, the revolutionaries and liberators of this century follow in their footsteps to win our second liberation. What was the bourgeois revolution based on Rousseau's *Social Contract* will be the proletarian revolution based on Marx's *Capital*. But the soldier who will fight will be the same as before – the Latin American. When the moment for the battle for liberty comes the people must discover strength within themselves to resist oppression and break out of their wretched conditions. Anyone who imagines salvation will come from outside is pitifully mistaken. If Latin America had strength before to throw off Iberian domination, it will again be able to rise and throw off the chains which bind it to the imperialism of the North Americans. Bolívar's heirs are not the dictators and oligarchies who betrayed him and let him die in solitude, but the people of the continent who have never forgotten him and his generous dreams of unity, liberty and independence.

The new soldiers of the Latin American revolution will have to be much stronger than the ones who defeated the Spanish and Portuguese Empires, but they will come from the same mass. The American negro will be one of these soldiers, like the Indian from whom he differs only in that he was brought in chains from his own continent to serve as a slave in the Indian's continent. His part in the struggle for a socialist society is becoming more defined as a class struggle which separated the rich negro – who is whiter than the whitest white, as Fanon says – from the poor negro who is closer every day to his Latin American brothers. The soldier of this revolution can only be a son of that people which is now dreaming of its liberty all over Latin America.

Che's death was a terrible blow for revolutionaries everywhere, from Latin America to Lumumba's Africa and Van Troi's Asia. But this man who was a legend in his lifetime has now become part of history and lives on to show us new ways forward and inspire new dynamism. His death in combat was a dividing line between the people and tyranny. His sacrifice is showing imperialism what sort of soldier it will have to face in this continent of hope.

And that is why the United States is afraid. Afraid of the demographic explosion in this Latin America where more than half the people are less than twenty years old. Afraid of the non-conformism and rebelliousness which are breaking out everywhere.

Tyranny is baffled by Che's image because tyranny is old age and stupidity, and therefore tyranny tries to suppress this image and fails to understand that he has become the symbol for an idea, a force, a principle, a conscience.

Popular rebellion is breaking out once more to complete Bolívar's gigantic mission. And men are finding certainty behind new leaders in the same cause at Zapata, César Sandino, Camilo Torres and the greatest of them all, Guevara.

This is the example and the challenge. America cannot remain subjugated and humiliated and despoiled. He took up arms for America and shed his blood. For a free America!

Index

Abolition of slavery, FJ's grandfather and, 21–2; its effect on plantations, 30, 157; Pedro II and, 37n.; an inflammatory word, 70; Nabuco and, 140, 148; Church's attitude to, 152

Agrarian Reform: a Question of Conscience, 153–4

Agriculture (*see also* Animal husbandry), of North-East, 64–5, 80; crops, 73; grazing rights, 74; Rio Grande do Sul, 75; control by landlords, 79; in Maranhão, 81; opposition to change, 82, 124–5; undercultivation of land, 91; single-crop farming, 92, 95; agricultural cooperatives, 97; agrarian reform, 126–8, 130, 141, 144, 149, 163, 164; conference of agricultural workers, 142; the Church and agrarian problem, 152

Albuquerque, Diogo Velho Cavalcanti de, 158

Alcohol, *see* Cachaça

Alencar, Miguel Arraes de, and minimum salaries, 97; elected governor, 129; jailed, 129, 135; averts disaster, 138; his popular government, 162

Alves, General Justino, 135

Amorim, Ofélia, 132

Animal husbandry, *parceria*, 76; tax imposed by landlords, 79

Anthony of Egypt, St, *called* the Great, 19

Arbenz, Jácobo, 176

Army, the, and the Peasant League, 136–47; FJ challenges, 146

Arruda, Abdias de, 24

Arruda, Manoel Tertuliano Travassos de, 29; his prestige and property, 23; his family, 23–4; and the branded thieves, 24–5

Arruda, Nelson Pereira de, 137

Arson, 156–8

Artigas, José Gervasio, 19

Aureliano, Rodolfo, 139

Barata, Cipriano, 36

Barros, Colonel Luis de, 135

Batista, Fulgencio, 178

Beatos, 56

Bença Mãe, complete text of, 163–9

Bernardina, 22

184 Index

Bevilaqua, Clovis, his integrity, 42
Bezerra, Alarico, 137–8
Bolivár, Simón, 19, 104, 175, 180
Bonifácio, 19, 104
Bosch, Juan, 176
Brazil, historical note on, 7–8; peasant population, 69; *parceria*, 75; *cambão*, 79; *posseiros*, 80–81; and Netherlands, 87, 88; and Portugal, 87, 88, 94–5; constitution of, 104
Brizola, Leonel, 141, 142
Bruno, Father Arquimedes, 142

Cabral, Lt Colonel Nadir Toledo, 137
Cachaça, sugar plantations and production of, 60; consumption by peasants, 60–62, 66
Calheiros, Dr Rodrigues, 150
Camarão, Felipe, 87, 88
Cambão, definition of, 11–13; in North-East, 78; *fereiros* pay, 79; generalization of term, 79; abolition of, 100, 101; and the law, 100–101, 106; peasants encouraged to resist, 102–3, 106; Láo refuses to perform, 113–17; Paraíban peasants revolt against, 133–5
Camilo, Joaquim, 150
Camponês, 70
Caneca, Brother, 19, 36, 59; on civil liberty, 37–8
Cangaceiros, in North-East, 36; and rebellion, 56
Capangas, peasants and, 62–3, 167; at Prata Grande, 131; to defend *latifundio*, 145; landowners and, 146; FJ proposes disarmament of, 146
Capitalism, refinery-owners, 30; the law and, 43; and *parceira*, 73; Mexico and, 176; Cuba and capitalist democracy, 176; and socialism, 177
Casas, Bartolomé de las, 59
Castro, Fidel, 177, 178
Castro, Plácido de, 125
Catholicism, FJ and, 17; peasants', 55; and Peasant League, 149
Christianity, peasants and, 55; distortion of, 58; and revolt against oppression, 59; 'threat' against, 145
Church, the, and the peasant, 144; FJ challenges, 146; and Peasant League, 148–55, 162; and *latifundios*, 148, 149; divergent views of clergy, 149; complaints against, 153; *Pax in Terra*, 154; duty of, 154–5
Communications, effect of poor system of, 28; telephone wires cut, 136
Communism, FJ and, 139; Lott and, 141; Peasant League and, 150, 151, 162, 168–9
Conselheiro, António, 145
Coração, Gustavo, 154
Costa e Silva, General, 147
Cuauhtemoc, 19
Cuba, and the Peasant League, 96; anniversary of Revolution, 163; exceptional in Latin America, 176–7
Cunha, Euclides de, 51; on inhabitants of *sertão*, 89

Index

Cunha, Luis Regueira Carneira de, 137

Darió, Rubén, *nom-de-plume* of Sarmiento, Felix Rubén Garcia, q.v.
Death, child mortality, 97–8; of José de Mata, 119–20; of Manoel de Mata, 122–3; funeral at Mirí, 135; de Cunha murdered, 137; of Texeira, 143; of savage plantation-owner, 158–9; FJ threatened with, 159
Democracy, 145; in Latin America, 178
Department of Press and Propaganda, 40
Dias, Henrique, 87, 88
Disease, statistics on, 92; on the *latifundio*, 94
Disraeli, Benjamin, 1st Earl of Beaconsfield, 90
Drought, religious movements and, 56; and peasant migration, 65, 66, 81; goats and mules, 77

Economy, the, inflation, 7; sugar and, 30, 95; and International Monetary Fund, 138; Briaola defends, 142; US economic expansion, 177
Education, reading primers, 68; lack of, 69
Environment, transformation of, 31
Escola Superior de Guerra, 136
Estenssoro, Paz, 176
Evangelista, José, 150
Eviction, 125, 130

Factory workers, 53–4

Fanon, 181
FARENG, 145
Farias, General Cordeiro de, 131; becomes state-governor, 136; and national economic policy, 138; and the Peasant League, 142
Farmers' and Cattle-Breeders' Association of Pernambuco, 96–7
FARSUL, 145
Father, FJ's, his influence on his children, 17–18; his property, 27–8
Figuerdo, António Pedro de, 36
Fonsêca, Deodoro de, 7, 24
Francis of Assisi, Saint, 19
Freitas, Father Alípio de, 132

Galdino, António, 134–5
Golden Law, 21, 128
Goudim, State Governor Pedra, 135
Goulart, João, 7, 138, 176; exiled, 129; succeeds Quadros, 142; and the unions, 162, 163
Gouvéra, Fernando, 134
Grandfather, FJ's maternal, *see* Arruda, Manoel Tertuliano Travassos de
Grandfather, FJ's paternal, *see* Paula, Captain Francisco de
Grileiros, 81, 82
Guevara, Che (*prop.* Ernesto), 181

Horse, the, importance of, 25–6; horse thieves, 26
Hunger, 69, 144
Huss, John, 59

Illía, Arturo Umberto, 176
Illiteracy, 141
Imperialism, US, 176
Inquisition, the, 58

Jefferson, Thomas, on freedom, 146
Jesus Christ, 19, 58, 145, 146, 155
Joan of Arc, 19
John XXIII, Pope, 154
Juárez, Benito, 177
Juàzeiro, Father Cícero do, 56–7, 168
Julião, Francisco, and Peasant League, 8, 96, 104–12, 137–40; and his mother, 17; and his father, 17–18; attitude to money, 18; the lawyer, 18, 38–9, 41, 96–7, 105–6, 112; and radicalism, 18–19, 44–5; and his grandfather, 19–20, 27; schooldays, 33–5; university, 35; his social conscience, 35–6, 38, 41, 44, 174; influence of Marx on, 40; jailed, 40; and the peasants, 68, 99, 125–7, 132; his two objectives, 100; Mata appeals to, 122; and General Lott, 138–9; leads marches on Recife, 139–40; his letter to Minister of War, 144–7; his letter to the bishop, 152–3; investigates charges of arson, 156; threatened with death, 159; his *Bença Mãe*, 163; attitude to Latin America, 173–7

Kennedy, President John Fitzgerald, 128
Kennedy, Robert Francis, 128

Kubitschek de Oliveira, Juscelino, 7, 138

Labour, unpaid, 11–12, 29, 75, 77–8, 80; hours of, 29; and land-tenure system, 72; for cash wage, 80
Labourers, 100, 101
Lacerda, Carlos, 138
Lage, Father Francisco, 142, 152
Lampião, Virgulino, 52, 56–7, 145
Land, enclosure of, 76–7; let to tenants, 77–8; owned by *minifundiarios*, 82, 83; undercultivation of, 91; impoverishment of soil, 95; uncultivated during disputes, 107; private property and the peasant, 126–7; Peasant League and, 165–7
Landowners, effect of sugar refineries on, 30–32; and *parceria*, 73–7; and *foreiros*, 77–8; and *cambão*, 77–8, 80, 101; and peasants, 90–91, 107, 140, 161, 167; and minimum salaries, 97; and Peasant League, 100–101, 107–10, 143, 161; *prova técnica*, 109; and rents, 110–11, 125; and peasant resistance, 126, 134–5; invoke aid of army, 143; peasants kill unjust, 158–60; and refinery owners, 161
Land Settlement Company, 127
Latifundio, definition of, 11n.; culpability of, 12, 13; and *beatos*, 56; and the peasant, 58, 156; *cachaça* and, 62; in North-East, 65, 66, 69;

parceria, 76; hatred of, 79; and peasant migration, 81; and *minifundios*, 82; demand for liquidation of, 93, 162; Peasant League and, 95, 141, 149, 161, 162; absentee landlords, 102, 125; agrarian reform and, 128; reactionaries and, 136; Lott and, 141; FJ's indictment of, 145–6; triumph of, 147; the Church and, 152, 154; Mexican, 176

Latin America, FJ's attitude to, 173–4; need for action in, 174–5; reactionary influence in, 175; Mexico, 176, 177; Cuba, 176–7; democracy in, 178; USA and, 179, 181; first liberators of, 179–80; new soldiers of the revolution, 180–81

Law, the, protection against, 29; tax evasion, 31, 62; young lawyers, 38–9; corrupt lawyers, 40–42; judges, 43; need for reform, 43–4; the peasant and, 100, 101–2; injustice of, 104–5; Peasant League and, 104–12, 139, 167

Lei Aurea, 21

Lenin (*formerly* Ulyanov), Vladimir Ilyich, 19

Lima, Captain Barbosa, 24, 25

Lott, General Henrique Teixeira, 7; and FJ, 138–9; and Peasant League, 139, 144; presidential candidate, 140; Sampaio defeats, 141; his ideals, 141

Lumumba, Patrice, 181

Maciel, António, 'O Conselheiro', 56

Madeiros, General Viriato de, 137

Magalhães, Agamemnon, 39

Malo Neto, João Cabral de, *Vida e Morte Severina*, 98–9

Martí, José, 175, 180

Martins, José, 146

Marx, Karl, FJ reads, 40; and religion, 58; landowners' attitude to, 145

Marxism, Lott and, 139; *Das Kapital*, 180

MASTER, 142

May Day festivities, 140

Mexico, 176, 177

Military, the, peasants and, 62–3

Military Institute, Brazil, 179

Minifundios, 82–3

Nabuco, Joaquim, 21, 140; on abolition and the Church, 148

Negreiros, Vidal de, 87, 88

Negro, the American, 180–81

Negro, Joaquim, and abolition, 70

Netherlands, Brazil and, 87, 88

Neto, João Pinheiro, 163

Neto, Soriano, 41

North-East Brazil, social conditions, 35–6; protest in, 36; slavery, 64; geography, 64; agriculture, 64–5; *mata*, 64, 65, 66; *agreste*, 64, 65, 73, 74; *sertão*, 64, 65, 89; peasants of, 65–7, 69; *cambão*, 78, 79; *posseiros*, 80; historical note on, 87–8; contrasts, 89; wealth and poverty, 90–94; proposed secession of, 87–8; overall conditions, 88–9, 94; cause of

Index

North-East Brazil (contd)
emergence of Peasant League
in, 94–5; child mortality, 97,
98; Galiléia plantation, 97, 98,
125–30; Prata Grande affair,
130–33; Paraíba peasants revolt,
133–5; Vitória under siege,
137–8; bishop denounces
misery of, 152; and Latin
America, 173

O'Higgins, Bernardo, 19
Oliveira, Franklin de, 92

Pacificism, 133
Passas, Gabriel, 164
Paul, Saint, 19, 154
Paula, Captain Francisco de, his
land and slaves, 19–22;
attitude to abolition, 21–2;
death, 22–3; FJ's attitude to, 27
Pax in Terra encyclical, 154
Peasant League, 70; historical
note, 7, 8; and the law, 71,
104–12; *latifundiários* and, 72;
first president of, 77; and
demand for reform, 93; causes
of emergence of, 94–5; and
latifundios, 95, 141, 149, 161;
its aims, 96, 163; beginnings of,
96–7; composition of, 100;
landowners and, 100–101, 130;
and individual resistance,
113–23; and collective
resistance, 124–35; increasing
solidarity of, 132; and the
army, 136–47; de Farias and,
136–7; incident at Vitória,
137–8; Lott and, 139, 140, 144;
convention at Recife, 139–40;
and the Church, 148–55;

Protestant leaders of, 150; at
Jaboatão, 150–51; the press and,
156, 157; charged with arson,
156; becomes subversive, 158;
blamed for murders, 158; in
Pernambuco, 162; campaign to
destroy, 162; and the unions,
162–8; and land, 165–7
Peasants (*see also Camponês*),
49–57; unpaid labour, 11–12,
80; relationship with master,
29; of thirty years ago, 31–2;
administradores, 32; and the
law, 43–4, 100, 101–2, 108,
167; life and mentality of,
50–51; tracking, 51–2; hearing,
52; and the land, 53–4, 55, 67;
and religion, 55, 56–7, 59–60,
148; *latifundistas*, 58; and
cachaça, 60–62; and violent
authority, 62–3; in North-East,
65, 66–7; *brejeiro*, 66; language,
67; population, 69;
classifications of, 69;
camponês, 70; an ideological
term, 71; *latifundiários*, 71–2;
Brazilian, 72; *parceiros*, 73–7;
posseiros, 80–82;
minifundiários, 82, 83; and
landowners, 90–91, 158–60,
161, 167; disease, 94; and death
of children, 97–8; of Galiléia,
99; urged to accept poverty,
101; and *cambão*, 102–3;
timidity of, 108; examples of
peasant resistance, 113–23; at
Prata Grande, 130–32; revolt
of Paraíban, 133; and May
Day festivities, 140;
demonstration march by
foreiros, 140; Lott's attitude to,

141; and the army, 142–3; FJ's plea on behalf of, 144–7; and burning of cane fields, 158; justice and revenge, 158–61; FJ's advice to, 166–9

Peasants' Charter for Freedom, 105–6

Pedro I, emperor of Brazil, 104

Pedro II, emperor of Brazil, 24n., 37 and n.

Peixoto, Floriano, 7, 24, 144

Pius XI, Pope, 152

Planters, sugar, effect of abolition on, 22; relationship between tenants and, 28–30, 32; plight of, 30–32; refineries and plantation-owners, 157

Poetry of North-East, 64

Police, protection against, 29; political, 40; and the peasants, 62–3, 107, 135, 167; corruption, 81, 121–2; landowners use, 101; reactionary, 102; on Galiléia plantation, 128–9; Sabino, 131; state governor's, 139; army and, 142

Pompeia, Raoul, 33

Population, peasant, 69; increase in, 92; of North-East, 93

Porfírio, José, 82

Portugal, Brazil and, 87, 88, 94–5

Poverty, in North-East, 65, 93–4; starvation-level life, 69; in Latin America, 90; and child mortality, 98; peasants urged to accept, 101

Prada, González, on Peru, 93

Prado, Caio, and the term 'peasant', 72

Prazeres, Captain, 137

Prestes, Luiz Carlos, 40

Priests, reactionary, 102, 103, 150; and peasant rebellion, 148; attitude to slavery, 148; attitude to Peasant League, 149

Protestantism, and the League, 149–50; Protestant peasant at Jaboatão, 150–51; and agrarian problem, 152

Punishment, of horse thieves, 26; 'service days', 29; for demanding *cambão*, 100–101; eviction, 102, 107, 111; imprisonment, 102, 107; for perjury, 108; of *capangas*, 133–4

Quadros, Jánio, 7, 141, 142

Queiroz, Colonel João Pessoa de, 132

Quintas, Professor Amaro, 36–7

Radicalism, FJ defines, 18–19

Ramos, Rui, 142

Refinery owners, and landowners, 30–31; in North-East, 65; arson by, 157; Peasant League and, 161

Rêgo, José Lins do, 30

Religion, *beatos*, 56; and the peasants, 56–7, 148, 166; purpose of, 58; and rebellion, 59; Winstanley on, 59

Rent, FJ's grandfather and, 20; proof of payment of, 29; increases in, 32, 102, 118; *administrador*, 32; *parceria*, 73–7; *fôro*, 77–8; *meação*, 78–9; unpaid labour, 80; FJ's attitude to increase in, 100; receipts for, 110–11; absentee landlord collects, 125; suspension of, 127

Resistance, examples of individual, 113–23; collective, 124–35
Ribeiro Coutinho family, 134–5
Roa, Raul, 178
Rodrigues, José, 154
Rosa, Guimaraes, 98, 117
Rousseau, Jean-Jacques, 180
Rubber, 125
Rulfo, Juan, 117

Sá, Captain Jesus Jardim de, 136–7
Sabino, Lieutenant, 131
Sampaio, Cid, and Kennedy's visit, 128; breaks his pledge, 128–9; defeats Lott, 141
San Martín, José de, 19
Sandino, César, 181
Santos, Felipe dos, 145
Sarmiento, Felix Rubén Garcia, 51
Sebastian Saint, festival of, 23
Sectarianism, FJ defines, 18–19
Silva, Manoel, 154
Silvino, António, 52n., 145
Slavery (*see also* Abolition), abolition of, 21–2; Brazil maintained by, 104; anniversary of abolition, 140; the Church and slave-owners, 148
Slaves, commercial value, 25; possessions of, 26; *foreiros* and, 77; in rebellion, 95; the army and, 139
Socialism, Cuba and, 176; and capitalism, 177
Socrates, 19
Sodré, Nelson Werneck, 124
Soviet Union, socialism, 177; supports peaceful co-existence, 178
Space achievement, 178
Strikes, and unions, 165; and the peasant, 168
Sucre, Antonio José de, 19
Sugar, plantations, 20–21, 27–31; prices, 28; refineries, 30, 157, 161; plantation sugar, 30; in North-East, 64–5; rum distilling, 60; sugar-cane industry and rebellion, 87; Europe and, 93; sugar-production and the land, 94; and the economy, 95; arson in the cane fields, 156–8
Sugar planters, *see* Planters
SUPRA, 163

Tenants, unpaid labour, 12, 19; three categories of, 28; rents, 29, 32, 110; voting rights, 32; in North-East, 65; *foreiros*, 77–9; landlords and, 80, 101; and Peasant League, 100; tenancies in dispute, 107; *prova técnica*, 109; on Galiléia plantation, 129
Teixeira children, the, 143
Teixeira, Elisabete, 132, 143
Teixeira, João Pedro, 143, 146, 150, 164
Third World, 177–8
Tillich, Professor Paul, on Christian love, 153
Tiradentes (*prop.* J. José da Silva), 19, 43, 175
Tito, Marshal (*prop.* Josip Broz), 7
Torres, Camilo, 181
Transport, *pau de arará*, 66
Tribuna da Imprensa, 139

Unions, organized, 162; Goulart and, 163; and Peasant League, 164–8; demands of, 165
United States, imperialism, 176, 179; capitalism, 177; and Third World, 177–8; and Latin America, 179, 181
USSR, socialism, 177; supports peaceful co-existence, 178

Van Troi, 180
Varejão, Aníbal, 137
Vargas, Getulio Dornelles, historical note on, 7; dictatorship of, 39, 97, 136; and justice, 146
Velho, Domingo Jorge, 95
Vidigal, Father, distorts Christ's words, 143

Vieira, Father António, 87, 88
Vieira, João Fernandes, 157
Vietnam War, 178
Vital, Veneziano, 138
Voting rights, 32

Wages, for 'non-obligatory' days' labour, 80; minimum salaries, 97; unions and, 164, 165
War, Minister of, FJ's open letter to, 143–7
Washington, George, 19
Winstanley, Gerard, 49–50; on religion and the social order, 59

Zapata, Emiliano, 181
Zezé, 128
Zumbi, 95, 145